Martyn Johnson was a 'beat bobby' with Sheffield City Police Force for seven years before he was seconded to CID. After two years, he found that he missed grass-roots policing and returned to the beat for a further seven years. He lives in Wentworth village, South Yorkshire, with his wife, Christine.

WHAT'S THA UP TO?

Memories of a Yorkshire Bobby

Martyn Johnson

SPHERE

First published in Great Britain in 2010 by Wharncliffe Local History,
an imprint of Pen & Sword Books Ltd
This edition published in 2011 by Sphere
Reprinted 2011, 2012 (twice), 2013

A CIP catalogue record for this book
is available from the British Library.

ISBN 978-0-7515-4777-1

Typeset in Goudy by M Rules
Printed and bound in Great Britain by
Clays Ltd, St Ives plc

Papers used by Sphere are from well-managed forests
and other responsible sources.

MIX
Paper from
responsible sources
FSC® C104740

Sphere
An imprint of
Little, Brown Book Group
100 Victoria Embankment
London EC4Y 0DY

An Hachette UK Company
www.hachette.co.uk

www.littlebrown.co.uk

For my wonderful wife, Christine, my children, Richard, Sally and Paul, who make me proud to be their dad, and all my grandchildren — six so far!

Contents

Introduction

When I look back at the early 1960s, I realise how lucky I was, not just working on the colourful streets of Attercliffe ('The Cliffe') and Darnall, but being shown around by and then working with some of the finest men I have ever met. The camaraderie was second to none and we were proud to work the beat and mix with different people. There was no political correctness. We just applied common sense and got on with the job.

I doubt if any of the men I worked with in the early days could hack the job today. I certainly couldn't. There are too many rules and regulations. The requirements needed to join the job now mean that none of us would have qualified anyway.

Without doubt they were the best days of my life and I made loads of friends – and one or two enemies. I've seen little ones I took across the road to school grow up, find good jobs and have families. I, like all the police lads, have seen sad and sometimes nasty things. Things that you try to forget but can't.

The pay in those days was poor, and there was no paid overtime. The job was more of a vocation. I remember when we were dealing with a nasty rape of an eight-year-old girl. Policemen from across the nation were ringing up, saying, 'It's my two days off – can I come and help?' Now that's dedication for you. In the mid-seventies there were strong rumours of a large pay increase and university graduates were joining the job for the pay and chances of promotion. Nothing wrong with either of those reasons but the job was altering and moving into a new age. The bobby on the beat was becoming surplus to requirements.

I'd joined the job to work with people and even after two years in the CID I elected to go back to the beat.

All policemen, coppers and bobbies have stories to tell about their individual times in the force. Some I'm sure will be better and most certainly different from mine, but I've never seen any written down by my contemporaries at The Cliffe. I, like all the other lads, have plenty of tales, so I set off to write some down for my own children, Richard, Sally and Paul, and also for my grandchildren, before memory fades.

*

Six years ago I was lucky enough to be invited to help Catherine Bailey with her research for Yorkshire's bestselling book of 2007 – and the most sought-after local library book of all time – *Black Diamonds*. Together we travelled several thousand miles over three years and she now refers to my wife Christine and me as her 'Northern Mum and Dad'. Catherine Bailey and Brian Elliott, my mate from our Radio Sheffield days, himself a local author and editor, urged me to put the stories into book form and I hope that you will find them interesting.

Special thanks are due to my old police colleague (but no relation!), Paul Johnson, an outstanding officer, and a true gentleman, for writing the afterword.

I would also like to express very special thanks to my dear wife, Christine, for all her help and support during the production of the draft manuscript.

I would further like to thank my old pals the other Attercliffe bobbies, and especially John Colley and his wife Christine. Thanks must also go to the people and the many friends I made in Sheffield – without them there would have been no book to write. I include amongst these: Pam, Ian, Janice and Brian Walker, Mr Dar and his lovely family, Mick Lee of Constant Security, Janice and Brian Smith, Mick Carey, Ann Loy and Robert Webster. My ninety-five-year-old mum, Esther, and sisters Bronnie and Elizabeth have always backed me up, along with my Radio Sheffield mates

Chris Mann, Brian Elliott, Steve Smith and Ray Hearne. In Wentworth I have been urged on by Angie and my girls at The Bistro; Dick and Heather; Sue and Steve; Richard; Erica; Steph; Julian; Jane; Chris; Rob; Nick; Big Ray; Big Andy; Mark; Ian; Spud; Lee; Andy; Debbie; Lorna; Cliff; Terry Corcoran; Clev; Ralph; Big John; Val; Darren; Tim; Jez; Dick; Malc and Kath; Graham; Derek; Philip; Adrian; David; Tom and Jeanette. If I have missed anyone, please accept my sincere apologies.

CHAPTER ONE

My Very First Prisoner

Squeak, squeak, squeak ... 'Am I hearing things or what?'.
Then nothing except the repetitive sound of Brown
Bailey's drop hammer about a mile away. The hammer was
used to reduce the size of the white-hot steel ingots produced
from the furnace. It was so big that when you were near the
steelworks you could feel the ground move.

There were hundreds of back-to-back dwellings around
Brown Bailey's, as well as long rows of terraced houses. It was
now about 1.30 in the early hours. How the families who
lived in these houses slept I'll never know. The big hammer
continued with awesome force all night long. No wonder a
lot of the poor kids were late for school in the morning.

Squeak, squeak, squeak ... there it was again, but this time
getting a bit louder, which suggested to me that whatever it

was, it was getting nearer. There were only two dim gas lights still lit on Stevenson Road and the only thing I could see was hundreds of snowflakes. It was 1962, the worst winter since 1947, and here I was covered in snow – hidden in a door 'hole', feeling, and looking like, a frozen statue. I had my night helmet on. Night helmets had a black badge on the front so as not to reflect the light, but there was no light to talk about and every time I shook my cape and helmet, the snow fell onto the three to four inches already accumulated on the floor.

I was reflecting that my first choice in life was to be an RAF fighter pilot, but having failed my one O Level at school, I became a bobby instead.

'All you need is common sense,' I was told – that's a laugh when you've no feeling below your waist and squeaking noises in your head.

The night shift had started at 11 pm, at Whitworth Lane Police Station, right in the heart of the east end of Sheffield – the huge industrial bit where anything could happen, and often did.

At nineteen I was the new boy, in age, experience (or lack of) and language. Darfield, near Barnsley, my place of birth, was only about twelve miles away, but my language was worlds apart from a Sheffielder's.

As I stood in the parade room at the rear of the 'nick', waiting for the duty sergeant, in walked big Albert Taylor, 6′

6″ and built like a brick s——house, with a craggy face and hands like number 10 shovels – 'Na den dee a da alright?' Another giant arrived in the form of PC Les Newsome. Quieter than Albert, he always wore a smile – but let that smile disappear and someone was going to get it. One by one they all arrived and bang on 11 pm in walked Sergeant Cyril Bowes. To me, at that time, he was very, very stern, and when he talked officially, like now, he somehow spread his lips a bit like a horse neighing, to reveal a set of yellow teeth. Sergeant Bowes was built like a Chieftain tank, so I never asked him why he appeared to snarl when talking. Besides, sergeants were gods in those days.

We all had our 'on foot beat' for the night and every twenty minutes we were required to be at a set point geographically: first, so that the sergeant knew where we should be if he wanted us; and secondly, for our own safety.

If we weren't there he could trace back to our last point to make sure we weren't dead or in trouble of any kind. A good idea, since there were no mobile phones or police radios then, only the occasional public phone we could use to summon help.

'Johnson, we've had a report that somebody's been nicking coal from the railway sidings on Stevenson Road. You keep observations there until 3 am and then, after meal, till 7 am – okay, lad?'

'Yes, Sergeant.' I daren't say 'Sarge' like some of the older men.

Helmet, cape, gloves, whistle, truncheon and police-issue torch (a steel oblong thing with a clear glass marble on the front and a clip to fasten it to your belt) – all ready. Pitch black and snowing like the clappers, down Old Hall Road, past Brown Bailey's Steelworks to Attercliffe Road, which was unusually quiet. During the day both pedestrian and vehicular traffic was tremendous. This was the main highway between the Steel City of Sheffield, two and a half miles up the road, and the adjoining large town of Rotherham, some two and a half miles in the opposite direction. The city boundary was Tinsley and there was no motorway between Sheffield and Leeds in those days.

I crossed Attercliffe Road, then down Newhall Road, with its steelworks all down the left-hand side and houses on the right. Half a mile later I was at Brightside Lane (not very aptly named) and then left into Stevenson Road. Both Brightside Lane and Stevenson Road were full of steelworks and scrap metal yards, much needed to supply the furnaces with raw materials.

The third time I heard squeak, squeak, squeak I realised I ought to investigate as it now seemed pretty close to me. As quietly as I could in the crunching snow, I slowly walked towards the noise, whilst trying to see through the blizzard that was stinging my eyes. I heard it again opposite me on the other side of the road. So, heart thumping, I crept across and there in front of me was an old-fashioned pram, of all things, standing on its own, up against a broken concrete slatted fence which ran the length of the railway sidings. What idiot was out on a night like this with a baby, and where was the mother? Only the pram was there and footprints in the snow made by whoever had abandoned it. The last time I had babysat was years ago and I wasn't looking forward to it this time, so when I looked in the pram and saw no baby or baby clothes I was relieved. So what was going off?

I was just thinking to myself that the wheels on the old pram would be brilliant on a trolley like we used to make as kids, when there was a crash like thunder right next to me. I nearly passed out with shock. With nerves jangling and heart thumping I turned and saw a pile of coal in the bottom of the metal pram – at that point I realized I'd got the coal thief! Every couple of minutes another pile landed in the pram, coming from over the top of the concrete fence. The adrenalin was now mounting, along with the mound of evidence in the pram.

Puffing and panting, a male figure appeared with his back to me, slowly sliding down the fence.

'You're under arrest for nicking coal, you are not obliged to say anything unless you wish to do so but anything you say will be taken down in writing and may be used in evidence.'

He couldn't say much as his arm was up his back and I had a stranglehold round his neck. Apart from drunks he was my first real prisoner and I wasn't about to let him leg it.

We were near one of the gas lamps, so I turned him round and got a shock. No hat, no teeth, no big coat, but grey hair, broken glasses and a face as pale as the driven snow we were standing in. He was frail but wiry, tears streaming down his cheeks and sobbing like a baby. It was forty-seven years ago but I can still see the look of despair and terror on his face. He was about seventy-five and ageing by the minute.

He admitted stealing the coal but said that it was the first time. Over the years, and after many arrests, I was to realise that they all said 'first time'. With a faltering voice he told me that his granddaughter lived nearby with a baby boy aged about two months. She had no money, no heat and no food and her husband was in prison; she had sent for her granddad because both her parents had died – he had bought her some food but couldn't afford any coal.

Naïve at nineteen? Definitely, but my gut feeling told me he was telling the truth. I had to pass his granddaughter's house on my way to the nick with him and I was torn – I wanted to prove to the sergeant that I could do the job, whilst at the same time thinking that with all those hundreds and hundreds of tons of coal lying there, someone must be nicking it on a much grander scale for them to even notice that any was missing in the first place. My man, I was sure, wasn't the coal thief we were after.

I'd just have to let the sergeant decide back at the nick. That's why he's got his stripes and I haven't, I thought.

The old man was starting to push the pram through the heavy snow in the direction of the nick and his granddaughter's house but he was struggling big style. I weighed up the situation: pram, with my evidence in it; old man; young man . . . and with that I grabbed the handle and started to push. I swear there were five tons of coal in that pram; it took me thirty minutes to get to Newhall Road where the going was easier.

From being frozen thirty minutes earlier I was now sweating like a stuck pig and to make it worse every time the wheels turned they went squeak, squeak. For a split second I panicked. What if the police saw us? Then I silently laughed to myself – I was the police!

We were now near his granddaughter's house and I began to wonder – what if?

Knocking on the door of the off-shot kitchen produced a cry, 'Granddad, is that you?'

'Yes, duck, let me in.' The door opened and there, framed in the light from a single bulb in the middle room, was a slip of a girl holding a baby wrapped in a grey army blanket. On seeing me she started to shake, while her granddad told her the tale and that he was under arrest for stealing coal. By this point she was crying and so was the baby. This set granddad off as he tried to comfort her. I could see a loaf, some milk, butter and a tin of Cow and Gate baby food in the kitchen; and a cheese sandwich was waiting to be eaten on the kitchen table, all the stuff that granddad had told me he had bought that day. The remains of a kitchen chair and some newly broken floorboards were near the fire which was nearly out. With their permission I checked the house further.

Baby clothes were in a pile near to where a mattress, covered with army blankets and a couple of army greatcoats, lay on the floor of a bedroom. In the other bedroom I could see that half of the floorboards were missing. I didn't need to ask where the bed and floorboards were, I already knew. What a sorry state they were in. There was an unwritten rule in Attercliffe, or The Cliffe as we called it: thieving for need and thieving for greed. For the latter there was no mercy but this was the former and, like a lot of other people in those days, they could do without a young sprog like me making things worse.

Back downstairs I went outside and opened the coal cellar grate, tipped the contents of the pram down the chute and went back into the house. There were more tears than I'd seen snowflakes when I told them that I'd seen nothing that night, but to keep their mouths shut. This time, however, there were tears of relief and joy as I quickly left the house.

Back at the nick I went in through the back door, grabbed my sandwiches and ate them in the garage, out of the way of Sergeant Bowes.

Bang on 7 am, I sneaked into the debriefing room to face him; the other lads had gone two minutes before.

'Any luck with the Stevenson Road job, Johnson?' he casually asked.

I daren't look at him and, trying to be equally as casual, said, 'No, Sergeant.'

'OK, lad, never mind. We're catching the same bus home, come on, I'll get my stuff from the sergeants' office.' With a huge sigh of relief I followed him like a lapdog. Once inside he shut the door and told me to sit down.

'Are you sure about tonight and Stevenson Road?'

'Yes, Sergeant,' I replied, but I knew I was somehow in deep trouble.

'At about 2 o'clock this morning, I came to check that you were okay. At the bottom of Newhall Road I heard a squeaking noise so I hid in the shadows. I could make out two people pushing a pram in the blizzard. I followed them to a house on Brompton Road where I then heard crying. I then saw you, of all people, come out and empty the contents of a pram down the cellar. Shortly after, you left the house, not to be seen again till 7 am. Right?'

'Right, Sergeant.' What would me mam and dad say – sacked after a few months? For the second time that night I was terrified.

'When you left, lad, I knocked on the door to find out what was happening, that's why you didn't see me at meal time. Eventually they told me the truth, Johnson, unlike you. I've been on the job a long time, lad, and I like to think

I've turned boys into men and policemen into coppers. Policemen have got brains but coppers have got common sense *and* brains. I checked the old man out, he's a First World War veteran on a small pension, no criminal record.' His lips curled up like a horse neighing, showing his yellow teeth. Then he said, 'So he must be *squeaky* clean.'

He then grabbed me by the ear and took me to a mirror.

'I'll give you a lift to your lodgings because they'll not let you on a bus looking like that.' My face was as black as the ace of spades and when I turned round he was laughing his head off. I realised he had never been going to catch the same bus as me.

He told me on the way home that all good coppers would have done the same as me and if I kept my nose clean I'd make a good copper. What a compliment, I couldn't believe it. When he dropped me off his last words were, 'By the way, Johnson, you can call me Sarge if you want.' I never did, I had too much respect for him to call him anything other than Sergeant.

Over the years I learnt a lot from Sergeant Bowes. In my book he was a proper 'mester'. A few years ago he went to that great nick in the sky and, as well as bobbies, there were villains at his funeral who'd come to say cheerio to a man we all respected.

I'd arranged to meet my dad, Fred, at 10 am in Tinsley. He didn't drive and I didn't know what he wanted to see me about. As I waited I realised that granddad and granddaughter would be keeping an appointment I'd made for them at the Social Security office, where I hoped they would get their problems sorted out.

A hooter pipped and on turning round I saw my dad in the passenger seat of a small lorry. The lorry was being driven by 'Old Jack', his mate. They both worked down the pit at Houghton Main.

'Tek us to where that little lass lives wit baby and no coil, will tha? We're in a hurry,' said Jack. Now it dawned on me. When I'd told my dad the story and about the appointment I'd made for granddad and granddaughter, he'd asked me what time it was. Knowing they would not be in, he'd arranged with Jack to be at the house to deliver about two tons of the best coal in Yorkshire. It would be down the chute in minutes, courtesy of Houghton Main Colliery – or was it? I daren't ask. 'Nobdy should be bart coil in this weather, especially a lass wi' a bairn,' explained Dad.

By 11 am, they'd been and gone – they had to go to bed ready for the night shift. So thanks, Dad.

Still nineteen, still naïve, but slowly learning.

CHAPTER TWO

The City Beckons

'Tallest on the left, shortest on the right.' All of us new and probationer constables were on the flat roof of Castle Green police headquarters in the centre of Sheffield, waiting to be told to which division we were going to be allocated.

'A' Division was police headquarters – later to be called 'The Wendy House', full of gaffers and admin staff. They wouldn't want me there.

'B' Division was the city centre. I'd only been to Sheffield once before – there were that many people it made me claustrophobic. I was more used to woods and large open spaces. 'Please don't put me here,' I silently prayed.

'C' Division was Attercliffe – I'd never heard of it.

'D' Division was Woodseats – again, never heard of it.

'E' Division was Hillsborough – even I had heard of that name, though I was not into football. I knew that's where Sheffield Wednesday played.

'F' Division was road traffic, with their Wolseley cars and the mounted police section. I knew they wouldn't want me there, as driving a police car was a specialist job and horses were for cowboys and Indians as far as I was concerned.

It looked like being B, C, D or E for me – but which one? I'd kept in the background and listened to the others talking. My mum, Esther, used to say, 'You'll never learn anything when you're talking, only when you're listening.' She was right, too, it was interesting to listen to the others talk. Most of them wanted the city, some Woodseats and a few Hillsborough. Not one said Attercliffe and I was soon to find out why.

Here we go.

'Line up, lads, get a move on,' said the chief inspector. At 6' 6" I was third in line, talk about nerve-racking. My turn. Looking me up and down he said, 'Can you fight, lad?' My job before this was as a blacksmith – not an ounce of fat on me and as fit and strong as a butcher's dog. I did a lot of weight training and wrestling in those days and I was solid muscle, so even though I couldn't box I replied, 'Yes, sir.' With a wry smile he said, 'Good, we've got someone for Attercliffe then. Good luck.'

It was not in my nature to fight, I'd been taught not to,

but I soon learnt that all this was about to change – by necessity.

The police had found lodgings for me in an area of the city called Handsworth, and I hated the place. It was filthy and matted with dog hairs. On days off I'd go back home and Mum wanted to know why I washed a cup and plate straight from the cupboard. The lady, if you can call her that, always had black hands, and her apron was the same colour. To begin with I wrongly assumed that I had to stay there because the police had vetted the place. But after a while, and after a plate of eight chips and one small sausage covered in dozens of dog hairs, I'd had enough and found my own digs. I was out of there like a shot.

My first shift was at night, starting at 11 pm and, after finding the police station, I was told that I would be attached to big Roy Sharman, who was going to show me round. Roy's nickname was Lurch, because of his loping gait.

'From Barnsley, I'm told. I hope you've got your booits on and yer ferret down your trousers?' Roy was an ordinary guy and we got on well together from day one.

As we walked up The Cliffe to our first point, the police box – or Tardis as they are now referred to – at the corner of Staniforth Road, Roy began talking. 'Forget what you learnt on that three-month training course at Harrogate. All those rules and regulations don't work down here at The Cliffe. Just use your loaf and you'll be okay. If you earn respect you'll get it back, if you don't you've had it.' I was to find that these were wise words indeed.

The Cliffe was surreal to me: hundreds of people turning out of the pubs on this half-mile stretch, men with flat caps on and white sweat towels round their necks, straight to the pub from finishing work at 10 pm. They filled up with ale to replace all the liquid they'd lost while sweating all afternoon – smelting and pouring the white-hot steel from the furnace into moulds or ingots.

There were young men with duck's arse (or DA) haircuts and large quiffs at the front; spivs with trilby hats and yellow scarves; and girls dressed up to the nines. It was like another world to me and I was mesmerised by it all.

As we got to our first point, the phone in the police box was ringing and Roy took the call by opening the flap on the outside of the box. Roy's head nodded a couple of times and the phone went down.

'Come on, we've got a scrap on at Ripon Street. I'll bet I know who it is. It'll be Wag and his lad again, they're always at it on a weekend.' We turned right onto Ripon Street, a fairly long and badly lit street leading to yet more steelworks.

'Don't rush, it could be over with soon,' said Roy.

I looked at the numbers on the doors to see where we were in case he was right. He had told me the number of the house where Wag lived and it was all quiet.

We were just about to pass the front window when there was an almighty crash of breaking glass, followed by a man flying through the window and landing on the cobblestone road in front of the house. The guy picked himself up and shook his head, which was covered in blood. Back up the alleyway to the rear of the house he went, followed by Roy and me – I'd made sure I was last. I couldn't believe what I'd just seen. We arrived in the house just in time to see the first man throw another man (his son, aged about twenty-five) through the same window that he himself had just exited. I thought at first they might be deaf and dumb because neither had uttered a word. The next instant the son came back in the house, also covered in blood, and his eyes were wild-looking. He grabbed a Staffordshire pot dog off the sideboard, smashed it and ran at his dad with the jagged bit aimed at his face. I was standing behind his dad when suddenly he ducked away, leaving me facing the jagged weapon. I had no time to think and, with the police-issue metal lamp in my right hand, I just straightened out my right arm and, bang on the button, he ran into it. His head rocked back, and he was out cold before he hit the floor.

'Don't let us have to come back here tonight, Wag. Get to bed. You both look like you need some beauty sleep.' Roy chuckled, and with that we were on our way.

'What about an ambulance?' I asked.

'No point,' he said. 'Ambulance wouldn't carry them and

the hospital wouldn't deal with them; they're a pain in the bleeding arse. Lad thinks he's good and his dad thinks he's better. One day with a bit of luck they'll kill each other and save us all a lot of trouble. They'll be okay tomorrow. You okay? You look a bit shook up. Let's have a fag.'

He was right. I was shook up and had trouble lighting my fag.

'That's adrenalin kicking in, kid; you'll be okay in a few minutes.' He started to laugh, and continued, 'Welcome to the real world – Attercliffe.'

We were back on Attercliffe Road now, just a few stragglers knocking about.

'All coppers are bastards. All coppers are bastards.'

Two lads of similar age to me were chanting from across the road, about twenty-five yards away.

'Na den, Bob, look at his shiny boots and new helmet – he's a bleeding rookie. What a ponce.'

I looked at Roy, not knowing what to do.

'They know we can't catch 'em from here, that's why they're brave. Look at their faces when they pass the lit-up display window of Banners' Shopping Arcade.'

I had a good look as they walked in the light and I already knew one was called Bob.

'Mark their card, son, they'll come eventually. They always do.'

A few minutes later the lads had gone and we had to

shake hands with every door handle at the front and back of every property on our beat, once before our meal and again after. This kept you on your toes all night. If a shopkeeper turned up and found his shop had been broken into and you'd not found it you were in deep water.

We all had set meal times which were staggered, so that there was always someone covering Attercliffe Road. Roy and I were part way through the meal when the office sergeant came into the mess room.

'Johnson, you're a strong lad. Jump in the patrol car with Les and Tony – PC Hardy has found a dead gypsy horse on Attercliffe Road.'

The patrol car was the divisional car covering an area about ten miles by five miles and looking after about 200,000 people, including those who were on the night shift.

'Jump in the back, young 'un,' said Les, and opened the door of a Hillman Husky Shooting Brake. Some patrol car!

'I wonder what he wants us for?' asked Tony.

'Especially with a rope,' Les replied.

'I've never seen him work the main road before, he always covers Firth Park area,' said Tony. 'He's due retirement in six months, after twenty-five years' service. Lovely bloke, but I don't think I've ever seen him laugh.'

PC Hardy looked like the Laughing Policeman you used to see in the amusement arcade at the seaside – but without the laugh. He was looking down at a medium-sized black and white mare which had died on the main road, at its junction with a small street.

'Pass me that rope from the back of the car, pal,' said PC Hardy, whilst at the same time apologising to Les and Tony for interrupting their meal.

I looked at Tony and Les and I could see from their faces that, like me, they wondered why we were here. By this time the rope was round the animal's neck.

'Right, lads, pull.' We all grabbed the rope and pulled the horse past Henry Wigfall's electrical shop, past a few more shops and then, just after the Carlton pub at the junction with Oakes Green, he told us to stop. Puffing and panting, we all looked at PC Hardy.

'Thanks for that, lads. I've contacted the knacker man to fetch it away. When they asked me where I was I couldn't see a street name on the wall. I'll ring 'em now and tell 'em we're at Attercliffe Road and Oakes Green junction.' His face was deadpan as he went to the police box to make the call.

We got back in the patrol car and didn't speak until we were inside.

'I can't believe that, Tony, can you?' said Les, shaking his head.

'They'll not believe us back at the nick,' replied Tony. 'That's one you'll never forget, Martyn.'

'But who'd believe tha?' said Les as he set off laughing.

By the time we got to the nick we were laughing hysterically – none of us could believe it had happened: pulling a dead horse about fifty yards because there was no street name on the wall of the street where it had died. As Tony said later, it was our fault – we should have asked the reason before we started pulling and not afterwards.

After finishing our meal, or 'snap' as it was known in local slang, we were back on the beat again and checking door handles. At about 5 am Roy turned into Worksop Road. After about 100 yards he turned into the well-lit open doorway of a newspaper shop near to Brown Bailey's Steelworks. The shop counter was piled high with newspapers, hundreds of them. Behind the counter was a slim oldish chap with grey hair – he was folding newspapers with one hand and was holding a cigarette with the other. Appearing from behind one of the piles of papers came a younger, rather plump woman who was also smoking. She looked straight at me and said, 'Sauce?' Before I could think what to say, I saw Roy nod at her and put one finger in the air. At that point the woman disappeared into another room, leaving me to wonder what was happening. By this point Roy was reading a paper whilst talking to the old man.

As I looked round the shop I could see that it was fairly small and cramped and it had bottles of pop, milk, loads of men's magazines, tobacco, Brylcreem, matches, fag papers and lots of other stuff for sale. I was still looking when in walked the woman with a steaming pint pot of tea (with one sugar as Roy had indicated), and a plate which she passed to me over the counter.

'Stand over there, duck, in the corner, or you'll get crushed.'

Roy was given the same as me and we both thanked her. What a gourmet treat that was to me (my snap earlier had been four slices of jam and dog hair). I opened up the sandwich – which was made of thick proper bread, not the rubbery rubbish of today – and revealed three rashers of crispy bacon, topped with HP brown sauce. The bread had been dipped in bacon fat. This was totally unexpected and I would have gladly paid my first week's wage for that sandwich. My wage, incidentally, was £10 4s.

I was still licking my lips when in walked a customer, a dapper little man wearing a suit.

'I'm late,' he said to the shopkeeper. 'Twenty Park Drive and a *Sporting Life*.'

The money went into a solid wooden drawer with dish-like cups which were full of change.

Roy looked at me. 'He's the local barber – opens up at 5.30 am.'

I thought he was kidding me but at the same time I realised that I could hear buses and an odd car or two and in walked another customer – wearing a flat hat and white sweat towel.

'Twenty Woodbines, duck, *Sporting Life* and [pointing with his finger] that magazine.' The newsagent put the girlie magazine inside the *Sporting Life* and, after paying, he was gone. One after another they came and after a few minutes people were queuing in the street. The piles of papers were getting smaller and smaller. We eased our way out of the corner and said thanks and cheerio – they were too busy to answer – and off we went back to Attercliffe Road.

There were people and buses everywhere going backwards and forwards between Sheffield and Rotherham and all points of the compass. At 6 am it got busier still. The night shift finished then, when the day shift arrived. Roy wasn't kidding about the barber. One man was already in the chair with the barber clipping away and about six or seven were waiting whilst reading their papers.

Over the years, Joan and Clem Johnson from the newsagent's became pals and on many an occasion when I was on night duty I'd deliver some of Clem's papers to allow him a rest.

Another newsagent I used to call in was on Attercliffe Common, next to the Lambpool pub. Albert and May, just like Joan and Clem, opened at 3 am, seven days a week. All four were fabulous people who would do anything for anyone.

Walking back to the nick to finish at 7 am made me think that everyone in England must work down The Cliffe. There were so many comings and goings. We were at the bottom of Old Hall Road by now and I suddenly heard one word: 'Ponce'. It was impossible to pick him out in the crowd, but I knew it was 'laddo' from earlier that night. He must live and work locally because he could not have had more than five hours' sleep. Time was on my side, he'd come eventually.

On the way home to my not-so-posh digs, with my first shift over, I wondered if I could last the next twenty-four years and 364 days before retirement.

When I went to bed that morning I couldn't sleep – the night's events were running through my mind. My thoughts went back to that bacon sarnie, the best bit of a night that I'll never forget; and then I went out like a light.

CHAPTER THREE

Johnny No Mates

When I was about seven years old I found a pot full of approximately 5,000 Roman coins in a builder's trench. It was located in the street in Darfield where I lived. When it was handed in, the builders got the glory and I got a clip off my dad for being in the trench in the first place. A policeman took charge of the coins and from then on I was hooked on both local and Roman history and also the police force. Little was I to know then that many years later I would have a regular fortnightly slot on BBC Radio Sheffield. The DJ, Tony Capstick, used to introduce me as Metal Detecting Martyn, and we had a right laugh, talking about my hobby of metal detecting, local history and some old police stories thrown in for good measure.

Two thousand years ago Attercliffe Road was part of the

great Roman road stretching from west to east. It started at Chester, crossing the River Noe at Brough, near Hope in Derbyshire, then into Sheffield and onwards to Rotherham via Attercliffe. From there the road split and one branch went to Doncaster and Hull. The other one went to York, known then as Eboracum. On top of Wincobank Hill was a Brigantian fort. The position of this posed a threat to the Roman cohorts and legions as they crossed the River Don. For this reason the Romans built a substantial fort at Templeborough and this area later became the boundary between Sheffield and Rotherham.

The Romans left our shores some 1,500 years ago and for centuries the people living in the Don Valley would have lived off the land and fished for eels and other fish in the River Don.

In medieval times Sheffield was famous for the thwittle, a large knife, and, of course, cutlery manufacturing. More work and workers began to pour into the city. As the manufacturers grew they became richer and some moved to what was then the beautiful village of Attercliffe with its clean air, thriving farms, windmills and orchards. Massive houses and halls were built, which in their turn required servants and workers' houses.

One of these impressive houses was Carbrook Hall, the home of Colonel Bright. Colonel Bright was a follower of Oliver Cromwell and took part in several battles on his behalf between 1640 and 1650. He mustered his troops from in and around Sheffield and they would have practised their marching and fighting skills in the Attercliffe area, prior to going into battle at places such as Selby. The Hall is now a pub and is said to be haunted by its famous owner, Colonel John Bright.

Attercliffe also had a macabre connection with the notorious highwayman Spence Broughton (c.1746–1792). He and his accomplice robbed the Sheffield and Rotherham mail coach and stole its post bags in 1791. He was caught the year after and hanged at York, then brought back to Sheffield. It was ordered that his body be chained to a gibbet on Clifton Street, outside the Yellow Lion pub, where it stayed for thirty-six years as a deterrent to other would-be highwaymen. I'm not sure what it would have done to trade at the time, although perhaps it proved to be of such morbid fascination that it brought a lot of business to the pub.

During the Industrial Revolution Sheffield's expansion was phenomenal. Virtually anything that was made of metal could be manufactured there, 'Made in Sheffield' becoming internationally famous. All this work required coal, labour, foundries and cottage industries known as the Little Mesters. The workers needed houses, shops to sustain them, schools and churches. Back-to-back houses were built in long rows in their thousands. They were cheap and lots could be packed into small spaces and, because there was no transport to speak of, they were built to make it easy to travel to and from work. People lived where they worked and every commodity that was required could be found in Attercliffe. It was like a city on the edge of a city. The size of shops like Banners attested to this, and the volume of shops and pubs showed how many people were dependent upon them. Picturesque Attercliffe had gone and was replaced with industry and housing on a grand scale.

As well as producing millionaires who, because of the pollution, had now gone to live on the other side of the city, it also gave birth to craftsmen and women who were proud of their work and rightly so. They were the best in the world and they knew it. There was such a diversity of trades, from dolliers to draughtsmen, smelters to stokers, founders to file-smiths, and yet they were all dependent upon one another for success.

Pollution in the form of soot and noise was something you lived with as part of your daily life in Attercliffe. I read somewhere that 500 tons of soot was deposited in a square mile of Attercliffe every week and that Brown Bailey's didn't smelt on Mondays to give the women a chance to wash the clothes and hang them out to dry without them getting dirty. The foul air would clag up your mouth and you could taste the iron.

This was the world in which I found myself in 1962 aged nineteen. No fields, no cows, no woods, no rabbits to snare and eat. An alien world to me and one which, for the first few weeks, I hated. After a while, and with the help of the finest coppers in the land, I started to enjoy it. They themselves had been there and they took me under their wings. Our very lives were often dependent on each other and the camaraderie between us all was quite simply incredible. Although I am passionate about my Darfield origins, I am more passionate about having been an Attercliffe bobby. The people of Darfield were predominantly coal miners, hardworking, friendly and generous. The people of Attercliffe were predominantly steelworkers and they too were hardworking, friendly and generous. I made lifelong friendships in Attercliffe but you had to earn them and sometimes in odd ways.

I'd been on the job now for three months and I was on the beat between Attercliffe and Darnall. It was about 1 pm on a Sunday afternoon, the sun rays were beating down and it was very hot. On either side of the cobbled road were men of different ages sitting or standing outside their front doors. Most were having a cigarette and a neighbourly chat, whilst at the same time quaffing ale from large jugs, recently dispensed from the off-licence down the road. What would I have given for one of those right then!

As I walked past the houses everyone was happy, they were away from their daily grind and enjoying their ale in the sun before Sunday dinner. There was plenty of good-natured banter which I took part in and gave some back. The atmosphere was great.

'It's that bleeding rookie again, Bob.' Two men had walked out from behind some old garages and were leaning on a derelict car on some wasteland.

'It's that ponce,' said the other lad very loudly whilst turning his head from side to side to look at the crowd that had begun to gather. Roy was right, they always come eventually. I crossed the road towards them, secretly wishing they'd run, but they didn't.

About a year before joining the job I was jumped on by four or five lads in Barnsley Bus Station. They were armed with bicycle chains and knuckledusters and they nearly killed me. I'd tasted pain in a big way and knew I was in for some more. Roy's words were ringing in my ears: 'If you earn respect you'll get it.' It was either them or me. They were squaring up now with fists clenched so I knew they weren't armed.

'You're all the same, you bastards, behind your silver buttons and your truncheons,' said Bob.

A woman's voice shouted, 'Shall I ring the police station for some help?'

'No thank you,' I replied, trying to sound confident.

We'd been taught self-defence and how to disable people by using pressure points at training school. Not wanting to be strangled with my own helmet chin strap, I took that and my tunic off and put them on the old car. I did the same with my truncheon and shirt, I didn't want blood on that.

As I'd been a blacksmith and done plenty of weight training I had a pretty good physique in those days and I could see from their eyes that they weren't as sure as before.

'Ponce is ready,' I said and they both rushed at me with fists flying. I rode a punch from the left and got a finger and thumb grip right at the back of the jaw where it hinges. I squeezed and he couldn't move for pain. The one on the right gave me a blow to the midriff, which was like iron then, and I managed to get a finger and thumb hold in his clavicle and squeezed. Neither could move so after about fifteen seconds I let go and pushed them backwards onto the floor. They looked scared now, but in front of a home crowd they scrambled up and came again. I took one on the left eyebrow, which swelled up later. I grabbed his arm and put him in an armlock, holding the back of his hair at the same time. The other laddo swung but I stopped the blow with my hand and then, foot behind his legs, I pushed them both on to the deck again. One lay on the floor but the other went to grab my truncheon off the old car.

A big chap jumped from the large crowd now gathered. 'He's not used it on de and da's not using it on him. He gaffered yer both fair and square – okay?'

Looking down at them you could see that they'd decided enough was enough. 'You're going to lock us up for assault now, aren't you?' said Bob. This caused the crowd to be silent for a few seconds.

'I don't think so, lads, no bones broken – let's have a fag and call it evens – okay?' The crowd clapped and some were slapping me on the back. Someone gave me a stool to sit on. When I got dressed and sat down the lads passed me a fag and apologised for their behaviour. Someone passed me a jug of beer which didn't even touch the sides.

The lads asked me my name and invited me to join them for a beer on my day off. After a chinwag with some of the crowd I thanked them for the beer and walked back towards the nick.

This took me down past the brickworks, then past Brown Bailey's offices and into Old Hall Road. At the corner of Fell Road was Mr Dar's tailor's shop and, even though it was Sunday afternoon, I could see he was working as usual. He waved when he saw me and beckoned me inside. Most of the lads used Mr Dar to make them a three-piece suit and if it was a rush job he could make one in a day. You could buy a good suit length in those days for £6 or £7 and Mr Dar would make it for, I think, about £10.

Having learned his trade in Pakistan, he had moved here about twelve months earlier with his wife and son. His English was quite good but his wife and son could speak hardly any. Mrs Dar brought me a cup of tea which they made with hot milk, just as we would make a latte coffee nowadays. Mr Dar asked me if I was married and when I asked him why, he told me that his son, aged about six, was behind at school with his English, reading and writing and they wanted someone with some spare time to help him. I was single and, not knowing anyone in Sheffield, also had the time. I nicknamed the lad Fred, my dad's name, and also my middle name. Fred was a lovely kid and a very quick learner and, in what seemed to me like no time at all, he was teaching his mum. There was no money involved. It was nice to be able to help such a lovely family.

I'd sometimes meet Mr Dar and his mate, Moonshine, for a beer and a game of cards in the Horse and Jockey and we've been pals ever since. A few years later when my wife Christine was expecting our first child Mr Dar's family were as excited as we were. Richard, our son, was born on 27 January 1971 and one of our first visits was from the Dar family. They were bearing gifts and a beautiful meal, somehow stacked on plates four or five high and all tied up in tea towels. I don't see him much these days but he's still working: a cracking guy and one of life's gentlemen.

When I was back at the nick for signing off at 3 pm, Sergeant Bowes looked at me and said, 'What's wrong with your eye, Johnson?' I could tell it had puffed up. 'Caught it on a cupboard door this morning, Sergeant.'

'Doesn't look too bad, lad – seems you missed out on a good scrap earlier. Shame that, we could have had a beer together,' and off he went showing his yellow teeth as he laughed, winked and nodded all at the same time. I never found out how he knew, but he did. He had an uncanny knack of knowing everything that went on.

Being new to Sheffield meant that the only people I knew were the lads at the nick and, because most were married, the only time we met socially was when we drew our pay packet on a Friday afternoon, and then we would go down to the Golden Ball on Attercliffe Road. They were a great bunch of guys, but there's always one on every shift – the 'boot-licker' or creep; the yes sir, no sir man. We were all in the parade room waiting to be paid when in walked the station head, Superintendent Rowe, whose hobby was ballroom dancing. PC Creep (for want of a better name) made a beeline for him.

'Excuse me, sir, can you do the St Bernard Waltz?'

'I can indeed, PC Creep,' replied the Superintendent.

'You must be very clever, sir. It looks very difficult. I wish I could do it.' The crafty old Super knew exactly what was going on and replied, 'I'll show you, PC Creep.' He grabbed him and waltzed him around the large parade room, winking at us all as he went past.

Finally, they stopped and the Super said, 'I think you've

been taught your lesson today, PC Creep,' and off he went to his office. The parade room was in uproar, everyone laughing except PC Creep, who had a very red face. The Super had stitched him up like a kipper and PC Creep was never allowed to forget it. For years afterwards he was nicknamed 'twinkle toes'.

I decided it was about time I took Bob and laddo up on their offer and on my way to meet them at the pub I called into the Chinese laundry in Attercliffe Road near Washford Bridge. In those days our police shirt collars were separate from our shirts and they had to be clean and starched. It was a busy little shop and everything was done by hand. When Mr Tsang did the collars, he filled an enamel mug with liquid starch, then, placing a collar on his knee, he would take a swig of starch from the mug and then spray the starch onto the collar in a fine mist from his mouth, at the same time pressing the collar with an iron; it was amazing. The collars were like razors but what his insides were like I can't imagine – but he kept a stiff upper lip!

The Queen's Head at the bottom of Shirland Lane was quite a busy and popular pub and for many years the landlord was Gerry Duggan, who bought the first Triumph Stag in Sheffield. The lads were in and standing at the bar with a couple of others. It was obvious that I was expected, because everyone in the pub stopped and looked at me. 'Get Mr

Johnson a pint please, he's with us,' said Bob's mate, whose name I later discovered was Keith.

The look that he gave to the other people in the pub said it all – he's with us so no trouble, okay? Everyone relaxed. We all had a few beers and a good laugh and talked about allsorts. Just before I left, Bob asked me a question in front of the others.

'Me and Keith both reckon that you could have probably given us both a good hiding the other day. Why didn't you hit us?'

'I know what taking a good hiding feels like and I've got scars to prove it. I don't wish you any harm so I didn't give you any,' I replied.

'I'd rather he'd thumped me,' said Keith. 'I couldn't move my jaw for four days, but it didn't stop me from supping.'

I used to see Bob and Keith in Attercliffe and Darnall when I was on the beat and we always had a natter and a good laugh together. We've been friends for nearly fifty years and every time I see Keith he gets on about his sore jaw, to which I reply, 'Shut up, you ponce, and sup your beer.'

CHAPTER FOUR

Peacock Had Us Stumped

The day shift started at 7 am and most of us had school crossing patrols to do in various parts of Attercliffe and the surrounding areas. There were no lollipop ladies in those days. My first time at this job was on Attercliffe Road where the kids crossed the main road on their way to Huntsman's Gardens School, named after Benjamin Huntsman.

Benjamin Huntsman (1704–76) was famous for founding Sheffield's industrial fortunes through the invention of the crucible steel process. His workshop was well known throughout Europe and his products were widely used. Nothing now survives of the industrial workplace that was the site of his extraordinary achievement. The name of the school comes from the green fields which were behind Huntsman's workplace and on which the school was built.

Most of the kids arrived early, with either mum or grandma and, because the road was so busy, they would wait at the side of the road and I would take them across in small groups. It was a good feeling for a young man in his long white gloves, stepping into the road and stopping the traffic. You'd tell the kids to cross and off they went to school. The mums and the kids were polite, nice and fairly well dressed. Some of them offered you a sweet. At first I always declined, thanking them for the offer. This would happen at about 8.30 am and then when it got to about 8.55 am the poorer kids would arrive, clothes not as good and looking as if they were straight out of bed and had had no breakfast. At 9 to 9.05 the 'late for school brigade' would come and these tended to be the ragtags from the poorest families, often pale-faced and undernourished. These turned out to be my favourite kids and they taught me a lesson. For ever after, when the better-off kids arrived early and offered me a sweet, I would thank them and take it, which pleased them, and when the latecomers arrived I would give the sweets to them.

'Thanks, Mr Policeman!' They couldn't believe their luck. The sweets went into their mouths and off they sped in a hopeless attempt to get to school on time. It was my first ever shot at public relations – I felt like Robin Hood, robbing the rich to give to the poor. A few years later I was to discover that my wife Christine went to that school and also took a sweet for the policeman. I'd like to think that he, like me, gave the sweet to a poorer kid. Most kids at Huntsman's Gardens School stayed for school dinners while mum and dad worked, so only one or two went home for dinner and then came back again for afternoon lessons, but some schools varied.

Over the years my main school crossing points were Huntsman's Gardens, Whitby Road School and Handsworth Road, where there were two schools using the same crossing. All three were on very busy main roads. For some reason most of the lads thought it was a boring job, but I loved every minute of it. You got to know all the kids and they got to know you, and over the years you'd watch them grow and turn into young men and women. If I had a pound for the number of people who came up to me and said, 'You used to take me across the road when I was little,' I would be fairly well off now.

The kids at Huntsman's Gardens were, perhaps, the less privileged, followed by Whitby Road and then Handsworth. Talking to the kids outside Huntsman's Gardens one day I was amazed to find out that some of them had never seen a field, a cow or a hen and had no idea where milk or eggs came from.

My uncle, Jack Jackson, had a dairy farm at Little Howbrook just at the other side of High Green, about seven miles away. A couple of teachers had cars and off we'd all go on a Sunday afternoon to the farm. The schoolkids loved to run in the meadows, picking buttercups and making daisy chains. They were allowed to collect eggs without lions stamped on them and watch the cows being milked. It was fantastic, after a couple of hours of laughter, to see them each carrying an egg wrapped in lots of newspaper, and a half-pint of creamy milk they'd been allowed to pour from the milk churn. They wanted to tell their mums and dads all about what they'd done. Over the years I've bumped into one or two of those kids, all grown up, and they say, 'Do you remember . . . ?'

What a character Uncle Jack was – hard as nails but as soft as a boat horse at times. He was a rough and ready Barnsley farmer who also kept and bred peacocks and peahens. They were his pride and joy and the kids thought they were fabulous. One afternoon I was in the police station when Sergeant Coulthard, the office sergeant, told me there was a personal telephone call, something not generally allowed. The office was surrounded by partition walling with a square opening where we stood to receive our instructions. On this occasion I was admitted but I could see that the sergeant was displeased as he passed me the phone.

'PC 656 Johnson speaking,' I said down the phone.

'Is that thee, Martyn? It's thi Uncle Jack here, cock.'

'What's up, Uncle?'

'I wonder if tha could happens ev a word wit' Chief

Constable of Sheffield like, one of mi peacocks 'as flown away and somb'dy's seen it flying t'wards Sheffield. Tell 'im that man at finds it al get a pint a beer o' two, okay?' Then the phone went dead.

Sergeant Coulthard looked at me in total disbelief when I related the conversation. He slowly shook his head. 'I've heard everything now, and I'll bet there isn't a copper in all Sheffield who'd know what a bloody peacock looks like anyway.'

I couldn't get out of that office quick enough, my sides were splitting and tears were running down my cheeks. I couldn't control myself for laughing.

Two hours later and I was typing up an accident report with one finger and still laughing.

'Johnson, you're wanted on the phone – again!' Sergeant Coulthard bellowed down the corridor. Back again to the office and I could tell from his face that it was Uncle Jack on the phone.

'PC 656 Johnson speaking.'

'It's thi Uncle Jack here, cock.'

'What's up, Uncle?'

'Will tha tell Chief Constable and t' lads thank you. A farmer on Halifax Road's rung me, he saw it fly in front er a lorry wi' steel on and he squeshed it all ort' road. I'll ev to goa, am upsetting misen. It wer mi best breedin' hen, tha knows.' I could hear him crying and the phone went dead.

I turned to look at Sergeant Coulthard. He was looking at

me and waiting to hear what was what. What with his stern face and Uncle Jack's dead peacock in my mind I just couldn't talk. First it was mirth and silent laughter, then it had to come out and I was laughing that much I was doubled up. He stared at me with his mouth open and then the hint of a smile, then he too started to laugh out loud.

The noise had brought the inspector into the office, and a couple of the lads. They looked at us both in amazement and asked why we were laughing. We, of course, couldn't tell them for roaring and slowly they all started laughing at us laughing. Three of the lads from the Criminal Investigation Department had heard the noise too and came in to investigate the strange goings-on. I could barely speak for laughing but eventually managed to tell the tale.

At which point one of them said, 'What's a peacock look like?' The office sergeant yelled, 'I told you they wouldn't know!' Wiping the tears of laughter from his eyes, he promptly fell off his chair. Laughter is certainly infectious because we all set off laughing yet again. The phones were ringing but no one could answer them. Uncle Jack and his poor dead peahen will never be forgotten.

The kids at Whitby Road School were older than those at Huntsman's Gardens but they were still nice and polite. Kids always remember the local policeman, just like their teachers, but you can't always remember them.

The school crossing patrol at Handsworth was very busy with traffic. As it was a dual carriageway you had to cross the kids from the pavement to the island in the middle, and then from there to the other pavement at the far side of the road.

This was my most regular school crossing in my early years. The kids and mums were great and I got to know a lot of them very well. There were very few kids who arrived late for school and I often ended up with a pocket full of odd sweets. There were more kids going home for their dinner than at the other schools and I used to tell the kids that I was also hungry but had nothing to eat. I didn't realise then that what, to me, was a bit of fun could be taken seriously by a child. One cold and snowy dinnertime I had seen the kids off home for dinner as usual and about forty minutes later I was waiting for them to come back to school. The first back, as usual, was young Sally and her mum. They were both smiling.

As we started to cross to the island in the middle of the road, mum said, 'Sally is worried that you have had no dinner to eat and she insisted that I bring you some,' and with that she placed a plate and a small flask on top of the Keep Left bollard. 'I'll be back in fifteen minutes for the empties.' I thanked Sally very much as she skipped away, smiling and waving as she went.

To the delight of the motorists and passers-by, I ate the

hot roast pork and stuffing sandwich wrapped in tinfoil and washed it down with a cup of tea. It made a lovely treat. As Sally's mum came back for the plate and flask I realised there was no washing-up either.

All good coppers had what we called 'cuppa tea stops', but when I first started I didn't know anyone, so how would I get one? A cunning plan was needed. At Handsworth you had a time gap of forty minutes in between the kids going home for dinner and then coming back to school. Forty minutes can be a long time standing in the cold without a fag and a cuppa. At one side of the zebra crossing was a small old-fashioned butcher's shop. I'd seen the two lads in the shop eyeing up the young mothers at the school crossing. I wonder if . . .? I thought to myself. The kids had just gone home for dinner and the shop was devoid of customers. Now's my chance. I walked straight into the shop and the two lads were at the counter.

'Can I buy a box of matches please?'

'We don't sell them, officer, we're a butcher's shop, but I've got some in my pocket. Do you want some?'

'If you don't mind,' I replied. 'I'm going to find somewhere quiet for a crafty fag before the kids come back.' With a look of relief, the eldest of the two said, 'We both smoke, come into the back kitchen where there's no meat and we'll put the kettle on as well.' Bingo! The plan had worked.

It's so long ago that I can only remember that one was

called Dennis, but they were both great guys. When the kids had crossed the road to go home they always shouted to me, 'The kettle's just boiled,' which was my invitation to a nice cuppa. My good hot cup of tea was often accompanied by a bacon or sausage sandwich. The lads were good to me and I made sure that every now and then I'd drop them off a packet of fags as a thank you.

I was just walking into the shop one dinner time when a chap in a car pulled up and wound his window down.

'There's been a bad accident down the road, officer – it's just happened.'

'Thanks,' I replied, and flagged down a car going in the direction of the accident. It wasn't far down Handsworth Road and near to the Cross Keys pub. I thanked the driver for the lift and walked across to the other carriageway, where a crowd had gathered. On my approach I could only see one vehicle – a large flat-back lorry carrying heavy steel bars was near the top of the hill. The driver was not in his cab. I enquired as to where he was and someone pointed to a man sitting on a chair outside the pub, in a state of deep shock, with his head in his hands. I confirmed that he was the driver and I asked him what had happened. He couldn't speak for sobbing and pointed towards the rear of the lorry where a few people were congregated. I walked down and the people moved to one side. There, lying face down in the road, was the body of an adult male whose head had

48

been run over by the heavy lorry. My mind was racing: had he tripped and fallen into the road or had he been pushed? If he had been pushed then it would be a murder inquiry. It was a horrible sight for anyone to see and I covered him up with a borrowed blanket.

Someone in the crowd said they had seen him walking up and down near the edge of the road an hour before. I went back to the lorry driver and took him into an empty room in the pub. He told me that he had been crawling up the hill with his heavy load when he saw the man on the pavement. The man had looked agitated. As his cab slowly passed him the driver saw, to his horror, that the man had thrown himself head first under the back wheels of the lorry.

It was later verified that the man had tried to take his own life on previous occasions, including once when he jumped in front of a car and ended up with a broken shoulder.

Poor man, poor relatives, poor lorry driver and poor me who had to clean up the mess – an experience that lives with you always. As a policeman I went on to see many horrible and difficult sights; it was part of the job. Some of them fade into unreality but the lorry driver had to live with this all his life and through no fault of his own.

Back to a more light-hearted moment. Fast forward a bit to one of the summers of the mid- to late 1980s. My local pub in Wentworth, the Rockingham Arms, had arranged a fun cricket match on the field behind the pub. The game had been set up by Scottish and Newcastle Brewery who leased 'The Rock', as we locals call it. The brewery team consisted mainly of pub landlords and management. The brewers were laying on free food and beer for both teams. For this reason there was no shortage of volunteer players for Wentworth. It was only a knockabout game so we didn't have whites or anything, just jeans and jumpers – but not Chris Kiddy. The landlord of The Rock was Lynn Ayscough, the best land-lady in the land, and Chris was her partner. He insisted on wearing his whites and, as captain, opened the batting for our side.

The cricket pitch couldn't have been more picturesque, the sun was shining on us and we had quite a few spectators. We were all looking forward to a few beers, a few laughs and a good cricket match; you can't beat the sound of leather on willow. What better way to spend a summer afternoon? We were all milling around the pavilion, where there were a fair number of people all anticipating a fun day. Chris won the toss and swaggered out to the wicket amid boos and jeers from both sides – he loved it.

Standing near to me was a youngish couple. The young man looked like a bodybuilder and a bit mean-looking with it, I thought. The girl, however, was stunningly attractive, with long brunette hair, and a fantastic figure. They didn't seem a pair to me, but odder still was the fact that she kept looking at me and smiling as if we knew each other.

A couple of minutes later there was a cheer – Chris had scored a four and was full of himself. At the same time I heard Mr Bodybuilder shout, 'Ready? Go now.' I couldn't believe what happened next. In a flash the glamorous girl stepped from in front of the pavilion, stripped off, apart from a G-string, and ran onto the pitch.

'What's going off?' I asked Mr Bodybuilder.

'She's a Boob-a-Gram, does office parties and stag nights. Someone's paid her to come and do a streak at the cricket match and I'm her minder.'

At this point she was near to Chris Kiddy. The bowler had bowled and everyone was shouting. Chris went for a slog and on missing slid down with his face on the girl's chest and then fell onto his wicket, knocking the stumps over at the same time.

The umpire, old Roy Chappell, shouted, 'Out!' but Chris was looking up from the floor with his mouth wide open. The girl bent down to pick him up, linked his arm in hers and, to great cheers, walked him back to the pavilion. His head was hanging but instead of looking down in the mouth for being out he had a huge grin on his face.

I was standing on the step with Mr Bodybuilder when they got back and she was totally unconcerned that everyone was looking at her – until she spotted me, that is.

'That was embarrassing,' she said.

'Don't be silly, you do it every day,' replied Mr Bodybuilder.

'If I'm right, I think that this gentleman was our local policeman at Whitby Road School when I was younger. He used to take us across the road. Now that is what *I* call embarrassing!' she said as she slowly got dressed.

'I'm sorry I didn't recognise you,' I said, feeling a bit silly.

'Well you wouldn't, would you? I didn't have any "equipment" then.'

She gave me a peck on the cheek and as she was going she shouted back, 'I bet you'll remember me next time though!' She was right. I can't remember who won but we had a great day. Chris gave a speech and awarded himself Man of the Match, saying that he was not bowled out but rather that he was bowled over – by a maiden.

CHAPTER FIVE

A Peaceful Night with Old Charlie

It was 11 pm and chucking it down with rain. I loved the night shift. There was time to think and, at times, relax a bit. I was on No. 7 Foot Beat which covered the Grimesthorpe area, about one-and-a-half to two miles from the busy activities at Attercliffe.

I'd worked this beat before and it was fairly compact, with not as many properties to check. On this particular night I started work at the designated point, the telephone box at the junction of Brightside Lane and Newhall Road. All payphone numbers in the city were recorded at whichever police station you were stationed at. Your route was normally chosen for you beforehand so that, in theory, they knew roughly where you should be. If you weren't there a search party would be sent to look for you. On the long Attercliffe

Road a police whistle or a truncheon tapping on the kerb edge could be heard in the middle of the night by the other policemen, who could come to your aid. Not so on the outlying beats, there was no one near you to help. The making of points every twenty minutes was, to some degree, our only safety net.

Standing in the telephone kiosk trying to keep dry was no good, as I had to make the next point up Carlisle Road. You could see lights flashing in the sky from the several steelworks all around me – smelting was an ongoing process. I was thankful for my heavy cape, which protected me from the rain somewhat, and hoped that my cheese sandwiches and banana, which were in the cape pocket, would keep dry until snap-time at about 3 am.

As I left the kiosk to go back into the rain I could see a young chap with no coat on, walking towards me.

'I've had a little accident in my car, officer. It skidded off the road in the heavy rain.'

'Are you hurt?' I asked.

'No, only a small cut on my cheek.'

'Where's the car now?'

'A couple of hundred yards away under the railway bridge,' he replied.

As we walked towards the bridge I was inwardly chuckling and thinking that this might turn out to be a good thing, as I could pass an hour sitting in his car out of the rain whilst taking a statement. The lad said that he'd been driving towards the city at the time of his mishap. The road at this point takes a deep dip under the iron girder bridge which carries the railway lines above it. As well as the dip, the road bends to the left. The footpaths on either side of the road are sloped with heavy tubular steel barriers set into the edge of the pavement to protect pedestrians.

We were at the bridge now and looking down into the road. I could see about eight to nine inches of rainwater, which had gathered in the dip. Even though I could see the left-hand bend of the road at the far side of the bridge there was no car to be seen.

'I thought you said that your car was under the bridge,' I said.

'It is,' he replied. 'Look.'

He pointed upwards above the pavement. I shone my torch and I could see a saloon car with its roof squashed and wedged fair and square in the underside of the girder bridge, about 15 feet above our heads. I just could not believe my eyes. 'Are you telling me that you've got out of that car with only that little cut on your face?' I asked.

'Yes, sir, as I hit the water it spun the car to the far side of the bridge and it hit those steel tubes. One of these pierced the passenger door, passenger seat and back seat and, because

I was spinning, it spiralled me up in the air like a corkscrew. I ended up up there. I managed to get out of a window and climb down the girder bridge.'

Looking from the other side of the bridge you could see the tubular railings twisted up in the air with the car suspended from them.

'Are you sure there are no passengers up there?'

'No, sir, only me.'

'A blessing then, because they would have been skewered to death without a doubt,' I said in shocked amazement.

The first question in my mind was whether the railway line was safe. Every time a train went over the unseen top of the bridge the car shook, and could have fallen to the pavement about fifteen feet below. I raced back to the phone box and rang for assistance. The divisional car (a Hillman Husky Shooting Brake) turned up with the inspector and sergeant followed by F-Division (Road Traffic).

'Well, Johnson, come on, lad. I can't see a car, where is it?' said Inspector Radford. When I shone my torch upwards to show them the car everyone's mouth opened in disbelief. 'How the —— —— has that got there? Close the road!' He was on the patrol car radio now, saying, 'Get the railway police down here and the police photographer – what – no, it's not a murder. No, it's not a fatal [pause], well, get him out of bloody bed then and down here now. Without photographs no one will believe it.'

'Right, lad, stretch your right arm out to your side and with your first finger outstretched touch your nose. Now bend down and pick up those coins off the floor and then walk in a straight line towards me.' When the lad had completed these tasks (there were no such things as breathalysers then) the inspector was satisfied that he wasn't drunk.

The police photographer arrived – I am sure he had his pyjamas on under his coat – and was amazed at the sight. He took photographs which were displayed in the police station for ages afterwards. Nobody had seen anything like it. F-Division had sent for lifting tackle to move the car but it was so difficult they had to send for specialist equipment to shift it safely. At that point in the proceedings the inspector told me to get back onto my beat and I left it with them; there was nothing else I could do. (The car was still there two days after the accident.)

It was now about 2 am and the heavy rain had turned to drizzle. I shook my cape, now weighty with rainwater, and off I went into the darkness. At the end of Newhall Road I walked up Carlisle Road to Grimesthorpe itself, where the terrace houses rose up to the top of the hill; then left up Botham Street, with the brickworks on the left and, crossing Cyclops Street, joined Grimesthorpe Road. I'd been up here before in the snow and spotted the tracks of a fox, or 'Old Charlie' as poachers and country folk describe him. I had heard about urban foxes, but I'd only ever seen the ones in the country. Grimesthorpe Road is a long road leading to the city and on the door of one of the houses was the number 656 – my collar number. I didn't know it then but some thirty years later I was to become big pals with a chap called Ian Walker, who was living at 656 Grimesthorpe Road with his mum and dad at the time of this story.

Across the road were some allotments and pigeon lofts and it was near here that I'd spotted the tracks in the snow a few months before. Suddenly there were cluckings and cooings everywhere. The hens on the allotments were panicking, which to me meant only one thing. Old Charlie, like me, was hungry and wanting his supper. I stood stock still in the entry between the houses and, sure enough, about a minute later, out popped Charlie, who turned out to be a scraggy-looking vixen with a hen in her mouth. Off she went down Botham Street. It was the right time of year for the vixen to have had cubs to feed. She was probably living near the old brick kilns for warmth.

About half an hour to snap-time. I had decided I was going to eat my sandwiches in the police box about 200 yards down the road from where I was. I stood in the entry and lit a fag. I was musing about Old Charlie. The fox was like me, he worked a night beat, and would travel many a mile in search of food. I was the same, but my search was for wrong-doers.

I was just about to leave the entry when I heard voices. Helmet off, so as not to be seen, I peeped round the corner of the wall. To my left, under the light from the gas lamp, I could see there were three young men walking towards me and each of them was carrying a large bag. I took off my heavy cape and put it on the floor of the entry. The last thing I needed was a restrictive garment covering my arms if there was to be any trouble. I put my helmet back on and stepped straight out in front of them. They were in their early twenties, one large and two medium-sized.

'It's three o'clock in the morning, where have you been?' All three started to speak together, a sure sign of nerves and panic. I looked at one of them, saying, 'Right, you, big fella, where have you been?'

'We've been playing cards in the city,' he said, whilst trying to be nonchalant.

I couldn't watch all three at once so again I directed my talking to the big guy. 'You must have won a lot of money with a large bag like that to carry it in. What's in the bag?'

'My football tackle. I've been playing this afternoon.'

I could tell by his face that he'd been up to no good and I was watching him like a hawk. The other two were still holding their bags with both hands, which gave me a chance. The big fella was the ringleader and I was watching his fists. 'Open it,' I said.

He bent down to do so and then, whack, something fairly heavy hit me on the side of the head. As I hit the deck, I could see two pairs of feet, both ready for running. I grabbed a foot firmly with my left hand and I heard him hit the floor hard. I scrambled up to see the big fella running away towards the city. The lad on the floor, who was moaning, had obviously smashed me on the head with his bag and, as he fell over, it looked as if his mate had tripped over him and also fallen. I couldn't get two men and three bags to the police box 200 yards away, so I quickly threw the bags and my helmet up the entry with my cape. I heard a dog with a deep bark nearby and shouted, 'Don't let the dog go yet, I've got them.' The lad on the floor was getting to his feet now, and the other lad was holding his shoulder, which he thought was dislocated. 'You're under arrest for assaulting a police officer. We are going to walk to the police box down here; anyone trying to run will have a police dog hung on his backside.' It was only a little lie but it did the trick.

We got to the police box without mishap and, unlocking the door, I pushed them inside and put the light on. All policemen were issued with a box key, which fitted every police box in Sheffield. The lad who'd whacked me had a real shiner on one eye, it looked as though his nose was broken and his lips like heavy-duty tyres, where he'd hit the pavement – oh, what a shame, I thought. The phone was a direct line back to the nick. 'Assistance needed at Grimesthorpe police box to bring in two prisoners, Sergeant.'

'I'll send someone. Hang on to 'em, lad,' the sergeant replied.

Within five minutes the two black Zephyr Zodiacs, with lights flashing, were with me. Luckily they'd still been at Brightside Lane, wondering how to get the car from under the bridge. Looking at the lad with the shiner and the other who was still holding his shoulder, and then at me, one of the officers said, 'Who's assaulted who?'

'I can honestly say that I never struck a blow – I was only pulling his leg!'

Back to the nick and they were placed separately in two of the four cells there. The cells were very old, just like the police station itself, and, believe me, they hadn't been built for comfort. Inside each cell was a very low toilet with two pieces of wood on either side of the pan itself. These served as the seat, and there was no lid. The walls of the cells were lined with ceramic bricks that could easily be cleaned. The bed, if you could call it that, was made of wooden planks, with a sloping pillow of wood. It was only about a foot high so that if a drunk fell off it, he didn't injure himself too much. How thoughtful. That was it, no heating or any other comforts. I'll bet they'd seen some action in their days. If I'd had to spend a winter's night in there, I would never have touched a drop again – honest. In fairness though, in my day, they were only holding cells, the main ones being in the city.

I told the story to the duty sergeant and to one of the lads from the Criminal Investigation Department. It was obvious that we needed to search the bags and I still needed my snap.

We arrived back at the scene in a brand new Morris Minor CID car and we could see something black lying in the middle of the road. 'What's that?' he asked. We were nearer now and I could see with amazement that it was my cape which I'd left up the entry just over an hour ago. How had it got there? The bags were larger than I had previously realised and when we opened them we found they were stuffed full of thousands of cigarettes. 'Bingo,' said the CID man. 'It looks as if you've caught two burglars.'

'There were three,' I replied. 'One got away.'

I picked up my helmet and went for my cape and sandwiches. If anyone has smelt a fox you'll know what I mean when I say they stink like a midden. Just like my cape did. The sandwiches were gone and I was left with a squashed banana. Old Charlie ate more than I did that night. Just as we were leaving I heard the 'police dog' bark and inwardly thanked him. I'd been lucky that night, I could have taken a real beating.

On passing the brickworks on Botham Street I shouted, 'Thanks, Charlie, and look after them cubs.' Mr CID laughed when I told him the story, and said that he'd never seen a fox. I made a mental note of that and about two years later I asked him if he still had not seen a fox and, when he replied that he hadn't, I said, 'Come on then, let me show you something.' We went up Staniforth Road and turned right onto Broad Oaks. At the bottom was a bridge leading over the railway line. It was breaking daylight when I said, 'Keep quiet and keep your eyes on that small island of land between the railway lines.' About fifteen minutes later we were rewarded with the sight of two half-grown cubs at play.

'Thanks for that, Martyn, I've waited all my life to see one of them,' he said.

Back to that night, though, and back at the nick. When faced with the evidence, the lads admitted to burglary of a newsagent's in the city and also grassed on the big fella. We fetched him in and later searched their houses. There were more cigarettes in them than at a newsagent's. They admitted to loads more jobs and were later sentenced to, as far as I can remember, eighteen months in prison apiece.

The CID man was full of praise. 'You would have done well to get one prisoner back to the nick on your own, never mind two, and it's turned out a good job – cleared up a lot of crime. I'm going to recommend you for a Chief Constable's Commendation. Well done!'

I was on cloud nine but starving hungry. Commendations were as rare as hen's teeth and in due time I *was* given a commendation by the Chief Constable – for keen observations and prompt action. I'd have liked to see Old Charlie's name mentioned as well as mine. Without me looking for him, I might never have seen the burglars and outfoxed them.

CHAPTER SIX

I Smell a Rat

Leaving home as a nineteen-year-old kid had been very difficult in the beginning. We were a close family and both my sisters, Bronnie and Elizabeth, cried when I left. Bronnie thought I'd be stabbed and Elizabeth, who was only nine, thought I'd be shot. For the first few weeks I went back home as often as I could, just to prove that I was still alive. For the first three weeks that I was away Elizabeth wouldn't eat and just clung to me every time I saw her. At fifty-six she's still the same and will often sit on my knee for a hug! I wouldn't swap either of my sisters for the whole world.

It took me ages to find my way around my patch. I had to get to know all the different bus routes I needed to use in order to get to the many varied beats in Attercliffe and surrounding areas. The main police station at Whitworth Lane was the one used to cover beats 7 to 14. The sub-station at Firth Park covered beats 1 to 6, Darnall sub-station covered Darnall and Handsworth (beats 15 to 20), whilst the sub-station on City Road at Manor Top covered beats 21 to 24. The last outlying station was at Woodhouse and covered beats 25 and 26.

Over the next seven years, before I went into the CID, I was to mainly work beats 7 to 24 and, after getting lost several times, eventually got the hang of it.

There were plenty of other new things to get my head around, too. A couple of times I'd picked up a fishcake and chips from Lomas's shop on Main Road. Back at my digs I would open the newspaper wrapping to find chips and what I would call a potato and fish scallop. I thought at the time that they must be deaf or daft in Sheffield. I'd noticed the same at Slack's bread shop on Staniforth Road. I had asked for a teacake and ended up with a currant breadcake. I couldn't reckon it up until another visit to Lomas's chip shop a while later.

'Chips and a fishcake please,' I asked. The girl was getting it wrong again, so I pointed to a fishcake in the top of the fryer. 'One of those there, love, please.'

'Oh! You want a rissole now instead? I'll bet you're from Barnsley. You have teacakes and currant teacakes there as well, don't you?' She was laughing away. I felt a bit of a twerp but she'd obviously come across it before, perhaps from other Barnsley missionaries to Sheffield.

It seemed longer than three weeks since I started at Attercliffe, but even though I was still a stranger, I was feeling a bit more at home. I have always loved people, especially the old ones. If you stopped and listened rather than talked you could learn so much from them. The people of Attercliffe and Darnall were okay in my book.

On this particular day I was working at the sub-station on Senior Road. It consisted of an office, a small room in which to eat, and a toilet. Adequate, I suppose, as there were only two or sometimes three of us working from there. It was 7.15 pm and I had just finished my snap. I remember it well: there was a knock on the door and on opening it I saw a young woman, looking rather distressed.

'I hope I've come to the right place,' she said, a little nervously.

I tried to relax her by smiling and saying, 'Don't worry, love, I'm sure you've come to the right place. Have you lost your purse or your dog?'

'No,' she said. 'I've just found my neighbour dead in bed – will you come please?' Now it was my turn to be nervous and I'm sure I was stuttering when I asked for her details. I knew plenty of the lads had dealt with only one or two sudden deaths in the whole of their service. Here I was faced with my first after only three weeks. (After that I seemed to cop for one every few weeks for the rest of my service.) I had no more idea than the man in the moon as to what to do next, so I rang the duty sergeant at the main nick and outlined the situation.

'Don't panic. I know that you're new, you can't be expected to know how to go on, I'll send one of the lads up.'

What a relief, I thought as I thanked him.

Ten minutes later we were joined by PC Garnett, who'd seen it all before. We walked the short distance to the house in Lister Street and entered. In the downstairs living room a large bed had replaced the other furniture. On the far side of the bed lay an infirm old lady, who was crying. Lying at the side of her was a large younger woman who appeared to be dead. No wonder the old lady, was so upset; losing a daughter must be bad enough but to have lain at the side of her for a few hours unable to do anything must have been horrendous. A few minutes later the local doctor arrived and certified death, but the cause would have to be ascertained in the morning by a post-mortem examination as he had not been treating her for any illness. Relatives had arrived by now and were comforting the old lady. It was pitiful to see and I was glad when we could leave. Tony (PC Garnett) had walked the 100 yards back to the sub-station for the divisional car and we were following the mortuary van, containing the body, to the mortuary.

When we were doing our training a few weeks earlier, we had been taken to the mortuary to see how it worked. There were, as far as I remember, eight of us and each one tried to be the last one in. There were two large rooms, one for the bank of fridges, where the dead bodies were, and the other room where the post-mortems were carried out. We were met by the two mortuary attendants. One of them explained: 'If you bring a body in during the day we deal with it, but if it's after 5.30 pm you are on your own. Get the key to the back gate from the charge office and return it when you've done. Place the body on this trolley and when you've found an empty fridge drawer, put the body in there with its name and address, your name, the name of the doctor who certified death and a brief description of the circumstances. OK?'

Neither of the men smiled, but who would with a job like theirs. The other chap opened the fridge drawers, which, I think, numbered sixteen. Apart from a woman with a plastic bag on her head, a suicide victim, they didn't look too bad. He then opened the last drawer – the victim of a road traffic accident, poor man. Half his head was missing.

'I'm going for my lunch now, lads,' he said as he pulled the drawer out a bit further. From the side of the torso he took out a bottle of milk and a plate of sandwiches covered in tinfoil. He then opened the pack of sandwiches and was about to bite into one when two of our lads keeled over and fainted. Two more ran into the yard and threw up, almost followed by a third – me.

I told this story to Tony and he laughed. 'They did that to me and all the other new lads. It's a plastic milk bottle and plastic sandwiches. It's probably the only laugh they get in a job like that or it may be their way of dealing with the pressures.'

We'd picked up the key so we went to the mortuary behind the Juvenile Court in Nursery Street, in the centre of Sheffield. The body was heavy and we both carried it in and put it on the trolley. Tony showed me how to fill in the paperwork and found us an empty fridge. 'Right,' said Tony, 'jack up the trolley and put her in the fridge, I'm outside having a fag.'

There was only a dim light bulb in this area and the fridges were humming. What with this and dealing with a dead body for the first time, it was really spooky. I managed to get the trolley to the right height in order to slide the tray with the body on into the fridge. I folded her arms over her chest and turned to open the fridge door when two things happened simultaneously. First, I received a hard slap on the back and then heard a loud moaning noise. I nearly hit the roof in terror. I thought it was Tony messing about but he was nowhere to be seen. I flew outside where he was still having a fag. 'T ... T ... Tony,' I stammered, and pointed back into the mortuary. Inside I told him what had happened and he laughed.

'The poor woman died in bed a few hours ago and *rigor mortis* is setting in. When you folded her arms and turned round, her arm swung back and slapped you on the back and she exhaled all the air in her lungs, which made her moan.' At that he fastened her wrists together and into the fridge she went. On the way back to Darnall I had a fag in both hands, I was so shaken up by it all. By the time Tony showed me how to fill in a sudden death report it was home time. I couldn't sleep that night for thinking about the poor old lady's sad loss. Her daughter had died of a heart attack at forty-seven years old.

A few weeks after this I managed to find some new lodgings with a fabulous old lady called May Proctor. She lived on Elmham Road, near to High Hazels Park, not far from Darnall sub-station and Darnall Terminus. It was just like being at home. The snap was great, the house was clean and I had a double bed. Mrs Proctor, which is what I always called her, was the nearest thing to my own mother that I could have ever wished for. She was kind-hearted, funny and she kept me in line. May was about seventy when I met her and she'd brought up ten children of her own and adopted two others for good measure.

Mrs Proctor would often tell the story about how, when she was a girl, in 1915, young pregnant women would meet outside the local paper shop for a natter. The main topic of conversation was how to avoid getting pregnant. One day the newsagent showed them an advert that had appeared in a national Sunday newspaper. It said to send a half-crown (12.5p, worth about £5.38 in today's money) postal order to discover how to avoid unwanted pregnancies. This caused great excitement, and over the next few weeks all the ladies put pennies and half-pennies into a tin at the shop. Half a crown was a lot of money, especially for poor people. When the half-crown target was reached the postal order was duly sent to an address in Harley Street, London, and the reply was eagerly anticipated.

After many days of anxious waiting the newsagent's wife called them together. A small parcel, addressed to her as arranged, had arrived that day. With great excitement they all met up at the shop at closing time. Chores and dinners had been forgotten – this was important stuff. The parcel was carefully opened to reveal a piece of white card. They unfolded the card and there written in large letters were just four words: KEEP LITTLE WILLY OUT. Most of the women there had worked in the cutlery trade as dolliers and buffers and knew how to express their dissatisfaction verbally. Mrs Proctor told me that in five minutes she heard and used a thousand swear words, after which time they all laughed. They had all been conned but appeased each other by laughing for weeks afterwards.

I was lucky, the Proctors were a very close-knit family, just like my own, and they adopted me into their lives. I lived there for the next seven years until I married and I loved every minute of it. Mrs Proctor had painful arthritis in her knees which were very swollen and it was extremely difficult for her to climb stairs, so her bedroom was in the front room, downstairs. May and Dot, her two daughters, kept our rooms clean and tidy. I can see Mrs Proctor now with her long pinny on, sitting in front of the coal fire with the back door wide open, even in winter. She used to bake loaf-shaped fruit cakes and these were her passion. She would think nothing of baking ten or twelve a week – only to give them all away. What I wouldn't give for one of those right now. She was also famous for her jams, particularly apricot flavour. May would buy dried apricots and soak them overnight and the next day magically turn them into the most delicious of preserves.

In the summer time especially, Mrs Proctor would complain about my sweaty feet and I didn't blame her. In those days we were poorly paid and couldn't afford leather-soled boots, only the rubber ones. During a shift you walked many a mile, which, obviously, made your feet pong. Washing my feet and changing my socks made no difference. They were so bad that when I took my socks off I had to open the window in my bedroom and put them on top of the bay window below. Believe me, they stank.

We both liked a laugh and one day when she was in the

kitchen, I stuffed a pair of sweaty socks under the bottom sheet of her bed with the pillow on top. The problem was that I forgot about them. Two days later I finished mornings at 3 pm and was back to my digs shortly afterwards. A chap dressed in a boiler suit was walking up the passage and I followed him right up to the back door of Mrs Proctor's house. He knocked and she came to the open door. 'How can I help you, missis?' he asked.

'I think we've got a dead rat in the house,' said Mrs Proctor, and she whispered to me that he was the local vermin man. She took him to the bedroom and, when I heard him say, 'That bugger's ripe, missis, worse than any dead rat I've ever smelt,' it hit me like a flash – my socks!

'Could it be in the cellar?' I said. When she showed him to the cellar door I grabbed my socks from under the sheet, ran upstairs and chucked them outside, on to the top of the bay window.

'Might be a break in the sewage pipe, missis. If it gets any worse I'll come back, but it's not a rat.' For days after, the house smelt of disinfectant but I daren't tell her until about three months later. Boy, did I get it in the neck, and quite right too.

Mrs Proctor was, to me, a mother, grandmother, aunt and sister all rolled into one and she helped me in my growing up, for which I will always be grateful. From knowing no one in Sheffield three months earlier, I now had a second family and a secure base. To this day I am still in contact with those of the family that are left, including Pauline (Mrs Proctor's granddaughter) and her husband Mick Spina – and Janice who was Mrs Proctor's niece and like a sister to me. Some members of the family lived or worked in the areas where I worked, as did some of the neighbours such as Bill and Irene Downes. This was fantastic for me as I could call in for a pot of tea and a chat whilst working the beat as well.

CHAPTER SEVEN

A Shot in the Dark

Some beats were larger and more spread out than others, mainly those in the outlying areas surrounding Attercliffe itself. For these we were issued with bicycles which were very heavy but had the benefit of three Sturmey Archer gears. Most of the lads thought they were okay but I preferred to walk. If you were on nights and riding your bike with the lights on, Burglar Bill could see you coming for miles – not ideal, but that was the only mode of transport we had then.

I used my bike as little as possible, but I remember one occasion I used it to go to my mate Pete's house, where I'd agreed to babysit while he and his wife went out for a couple of hours. On his return he drove me back to my digs – I clean forgot about my bike. The bikes were regularly inspected and, about a week later, the duty sergeant wanted to inspect mine, along with everyone else's. I'd left it in Pete's shed, so I went to pick it up.

As I arrived, his kids of six and eight returned from school. 'Uncle Martyn, we've cleaned your bike for you.' You could see that they were quite excited. I was musing to myself about how nice the kids were as I opened the shed door. There in front of me was my police bike. The kids were now in the shed, looking up at me and waiting for me to praise them for their hard work. I didn't know whether to laugh or cry – the bike frame had been painted pink and the wheels and saddle yellow! At this point, Pete came into the shed and went berserk at them and they promptly started to cry. When I told them that I thought the bike looked better than it did before, the smiles came back and I gave them a shilling each. They were over the moon.

Pete, also a copper, had more service in than me and was a bit more worldly wise. He got on the phone to the sergeant. 'There's been a spate of thefts of pedal cycles in this area over the last few weeks and the cheeky buggers have now nicked Martyn Johnson's out of my shed.' Pause . . .

'Yes, Sarge, I know who it is, I'm just waiting to catch them with a bike. Don't worry, I'll have em.' (Another pause.) 'Yes, Sarge, I'll tell him.' Down went the phone.

This is it, I thought, I'm in bother now.

'The sergeant isn't pleased about your bike going missing, but says that you are on a police motorcycle course starting at West Bar on Monday.' He began to laugh. 'You'll look a right fairy if it's pink and yellow like your old bike!'

Pete's daughter went on to become a very well-known fashion designer and I'd like to bet that painting my police bike was her first paid commission.

The motorcycle course was great. By this time the old Velocettes that they used in the filming of *Heartbeat* had been replaced by 250cc Ariel Leaders, which were both noisy and tinny but easy to use. The colour was black and white, thankfully. I'd have hated being called the Fairy Leader! The course was run by Sergeant Street and Sergeant Hill, who were both top-class drivers. In fact, Sergeant Street was so handy behind the wheel that he was once asked by the Chief Constable to give a running commentary to show off his driving and observation skills whilst driving a car full of dignitaries through the city.

He threaded his way through Sheffield, commentating on what he could see and how he would approach junctions, observing pedestrians and taking steps to avoid accidents; he commented on the way other people were driving too. He was a perfectionist and his driving and observations skills were second to none, and his passengers were suitably impressed.

At a certain point during the journey his commentary went as follows: 'At the next T-junction I will turn right into

Eccleshall Road, where I need to be aware of piles of elephant dung on the highway.' Apparently the Chief shuffled in his seat and thought his sergeant had gone mad ... until they turned into Eccleshall Road, where, sure enough, there was the odd large pile of elephant muck in the road. All, including the Chief, were amazed and extremely impressed at his skills of observation. Back at the station the Chief asked Sergeant Street how he did it, to which he replied, 'It was easy, sir. Reading the *Sheffield Star* last night I noticed that the circus was in town and would be parading down Eccleshall Road at 2.15 pm. I scheduled my drive to be there ten minutes afterwards and, as everyone knows, sir, elephants are very obliging creatures in certain departments. Luckily for me, sir, I was right.'

'Brilliant, Sergeant Street. They say that elephants never forget and neither will I,' and off he went, shaking his head and laughing to himself.

The police motorbikes were in use twenty-four hours a day and operated from the main police station at Whitworth Lane. The day-shift man would return the bike to the station at about 2.50 pm and, if you were the afternoon man, you would use the same gloves, goggles and even the same helmet that he'd been wearing (not very hygienic to say the least), and off you went to your respective beat on the outer reaches of the district. The motorbikes were equipped with a radio and handset, which was good unless you were in a poor reception area, and each bike had its own radio identity number. Because of the radio you didn't need to make twenty-minute points as you did on the beat, and this allowed you the freedom to work the area as you thought fit.

I enjoyed the freedom of it, especially on the night shift. If I was on the Woodhouse beat I would ride down to Woodhouse Mill, near to the River Rother, and enter another world. This was where I felt most at home. I was born about 100 yards from the River Dearne at its confluence with the River Dove at Darfield and it was very similar to Woodhouse Mill.

As dawn came up in the early summer months and the mist lightly covered the flowers in the meadows, the country-side would come to life. The barn owl slowly and silently flapped his wings, which were nearly touching the ground as he toured the meadow looking for food. The frogs and toads kept quiet as the heron strutted by, also looking for his break-fast. There were ducks, water rail and peewits (lapwings) in abundance and the songbirds sang their incredible dawn chorus of whistles, warbles and tweets. Young rabbits were everywhere, along with the odd leveret and mum or dad hare. I wanted the whole of Woodhouse to wake up and come and watch this fantastic free spectacle that nature had provided.

I turned towards Sheffield but all I could hear there was the city snoring.

It was about 5.30 am after what had been a fairly quiet

Saturday night. A few 'domestics' and that was it. I was making my way back towards Attercliffe and wondering why so many private buses were heading towards the city. They were from all over the place – Worksop, Harthill, Clowne. The buses had a card with a number on displayed in the front window and the name and address of the bus company on the rear doors. I was intrigued.

Darnall Terminus was alive with men, most of them with wicker baskets on their backs. Buses by the dozen were parked everywhere and a long queue snaked its way towards the fishing tackle shop near the Wellington pub. Crates of beer and fishing baskets were loaded into the multitude of buses along with maggots by the million; it was the annual works' fishing competition. I thought I heard somebody say that they were going to fish the Forty Foot Drain near Boston in Lincolnshire, but I couldn't clarify that because the radio on the bike was going crazy. 'Hello, four nine, come in, four nine.' When I answered, the controller said (I can still hear him saying it, even now), 'Go immediately to Tansley Street at Wincobank. A woman has been shot and the gunman has run into a nearby house. Some of the lads have finished early so you're on your own.'

The engine was screaming as I went down Greenland Road and I was going so fast that I nearly lost control over Broughton Lane Bridge. 'Slow down, idiot,' I said to myself. Then I began to think about the possibilities – what if he shoots at me? I could be killed. At that point I rode a bit slower for a couple of hundred yards. I was going to confront a gunman on my own and all I was wearing was a light tunic. 'Think, lad, think,' I said to myself. 'Padding over my heart, that's what I need.' I pulled the bike up and opened the panniers. Inside were wads of report forms and a clipboard. I shoved everything into the left-hand side of my tunic to cover my heart. I must have looked like the Michelin Man down my left side. It had only taken a few seconds but it made me feel guilty – a funny thing, fear.

I was travelling like the clappers now and my heart was racing. I was nearly there. I turned into Tansley Street and pulled up in front of a crowd of people who were standing around. Some were pointing to a nearby house and a chap, still in his pyjamas, told me that the gunman was in the rear of the house. I hadn't a clue what to expect so I adjusted the wads of papers in my tunic and drew my truncheon – for the first and only time.

The kitchen door was open and I could hear several voices coming from inside. I slowly put my head round the door frame and there, on the kitchen table, was a shotgun. To my relief I could see that it was opened and unloaded. There were three people in the room. Seated on a kitchen chair near the table was a young man of about twenty-six to twenty-eight years old. He was dressed in a camouflage jacket and his head was cupped in his hands. He was rocking backwards and forwards in the chair, a sure sign that he was in deep shock. The second was a white-haired old lady who was trying to comfort the young man, even though she was covered in blood and looked very, very pale. The third person in the room was a nurse who said she lived nearby. She had been called to the scene by neighbours.

On the table was a knife and fork so I hooked the knife under the trigger guard of the gun and took it outside, out of harm's way, whilst also preserving any fingerprint evidence. I'd asked the nurse to follow me to try and find out what had happened. 'All I know is that the young man has shot the old lady in the arm, they are both in shock and she needs urgent hospital treatment. I've done all I can with the wound but it's not good enough. She might die.'

My initial fears of a man waving a loaded gun at everybody were now dispelled. The old lady was the real priority. Back in the house she looked bad but was saying to the young man, 'Don't worry, duck, I know you didn't mean to do it – I'll be okay.' The ambulance had arrived by now and they took away the padding from the lady's arm. About three inches above her wrist was a hole about one by one-and-a-half inches across. What a mess. She must have been shot at fairly close range before the lead shot had had time to spread out. Within a minute or two the ambulance and the old lady were off to hospital. From my arrival to the ambulance leaving took less than five minutes and I was just hoping that she would survive.

I thanked the nurse for her help and, after getting her details in order to obtain a statement later, I closed the kitchen door behind her as she left. The young man was sobbing uncontrollably and mumbling, 'It was an accident, it was an accident. I just want to die.' I cautioned him and, after telling him that he was under arrest, asked him to tell me, in his own words, what had happened. Every word brought about another sob, he was in such torment that he was incoherent and I couldn't make out what he was saying.

The morning inspector and a detective arrived and the young man was taken to Attercliffe police station. A local doctor was asked to be in attendance on his arrival at the station, to check him out. The old lady's relatives had come to the house, so I quickly locked the door behind me and despatched them to the hospital. At this stage we didn't know what had happened. The house itself could have been the crime scene and contained evidence so I had to take extra care to make sure that nothing was disturbed. With the house key safely in my pocket, I told the neighbours that I would be back to talk to them later. I sped back to the police station. The doctor was there and gave the young man a sedative to calm him down, stating that he had no injuries and that we could interview him without a problem.

It was explained to him how serious his situation was and that if he wished he could have a solicitor present. 'No thank you, I've done wrong and I must pay for what I've done.' He went on to tell us that he often went out early on a Sunday morning with his shotgun (which was licensed) in the hope of bagging a couple of rabbits for dinner. He lived about two miles away and had previously noticed the odd rabbit or two on some wasteland on Wincobank Hill. There were quite a few bushes and trees on the land and he was slowly and quietly walking amongst them in the hope of flushing out a rabbit, when suddenly he saw something small and white move at ground level behind a nearby bush. Thinking it was a rabbit's tail he lifted his gun and fired. He then ran to the rear of the bush and at the same time heard the old lady scream. The lad found her on the ground holding her right arm with her left hand and he saw blood oozing through her white cardigan. He had obviously mistaken her white cardigan for the rabbit's tail. He picked her up and managed to get her back to her home and then banged on the neighbours' door asking for assistance. They in turn had rung 999 for the police and ambulance and also woken the nurse and asked her to come as quickly as possible. He said that the old lady had told him that she had been looking for blackberries.

The head of CID was on the phone to the inspector and wanted to know if it was a murder inquiry. When he knew the circumstances he told the detective to visit the hospital for a statement from the lady and an update as to her health. The young man had not intended to harm anyone but if the old lady were to die within a year and a day the charge would be serious: manslaughter.

I chatted with the young man whilst waiting for the hospital report. No previous convictions, a decent job, all in all a normal everyday sort of a guy, no malice or harm in him whatsoever. Because of this he wasn't in the cells and we just chatted whilst we waited for the news from the hospital. The news was inconclusive, it could go either way – we could only hope that it was the right way. Beside himself with worry, he was later bailed to appear back at the nick the following week. We didn't charge him with anything because the charge depended on whether the lady pulled through.

By this time I was whacked – it had been a long shift, but sleep didn't come easily. Questions were on my mind. Will she live? Should I have padded up when it turned out that I didn't need to? Was I a coward? When I received the call to attend the incident I had no idea what I might find there and I took the only precaution that I could take. It might have been a sniper shooting wildly, I wasn't to know. On reflection I think my actions were correct in shoving the padding into my tunic. After all, look at today's policemen. They are, and quite rightly so, kitted out with body armour, CS gas, tasers (electronic shock weapons) and suchlike, whereas I was on my own not knowing what to expect and armed only with a little bit of wood.

Fortunately, the old lady came through her ordeal and

lived for a good few years afterwards. I visited her from time to time when she was in hospital and after she had been discharged. The young man who accidentally shot her also visited her and took her flowers every now and then. I'll bet he took the biggest bunch one year and two days after the incident.

I've bumped into him a few times over the last forty-odd years and he never got over it. Two years ago I dropped someone off in the road where he lived and asked if they knew him. 'Yes, he's lived like a recluse for years, never married. Someone told me that he had a bad do with a woman years ago and it sent him a bit "doolally" – but he's totally harmless really.'

Life is, as we all know, full of 'ifs', but if he'd only have tried to snare the rabbit rather than shoot it, he might now have a normal life with a wife, children and grandchildren – poor man and poor old lady.

CHAPTER EIGHT

What's a Crash Course?

Traffic duty was something that you either loved or hated, but it had to be done. The sheer volume of traffic leaving the steelworks at tea time was enormous. When British Steel on Brightside Lane and The Admiralty on Bold Street disgorged their workforce – all at the same time – it created massive tailbacks all the way down Janson Street and you couldn't join Attercliffe Common because of the volume of traffic there. It was the same on Brightside Lane at the opposite end of Janson Street. These two junctions and the one at Attercliffe Road, where it met Staniforth Road, were the three main points where we worked traffic control at tea time.

By far the easiest junction to control was the one at Attercliffe Common and Janson Street. That is the one where I was taught, along with everyone else. When you were assigned to traffic duty you had to wear a long white coat and gloves and felt a bit like a conductor in an orchestra. You had to control both direction and speed. After a while and with practice you got more adept and the traffic flowed faster, which suited the car drivers who got home that little bit earlier.

For a few days I'd been teaching a new policewoman the art of traffic control. Not an easy thing as it can only be done by one person, so the pupil has to learn by observation. Although worried, she agreed to make a start on her own. I eased her in gently by starting fifteen minutes before the worst of the rush hour traffic began. She was doing fine and when the rush hour started she was all smiles and waving arms. I watched her for a further twenty minutes. Her confidence was growing by the minute and she was doing well. I shouted cheerio and off I went – we had previously agreed that if she was okay and felt confident to carry on without me, I'd leave her on her own for a while. I told her to take her time and not rush.

I'd walked for about five minutes back up The Cliffe when I heard a muffled bang, bang, bang behind me. Looking back down the road I could see, in the distance, that no cars were moving and the policewoman was nowhere to be seen. I raced back to the junction and could see that the traffic was now solid as far as the eye could see, in both directions on

Attercliffe Common and the same down Janson Street. I assessed the scene quickly and spotted the policewoman sitting on the kerb edge, crying. I established that she wasn't hurt and turned to see the minor wreckage of seven cars spread across the junction. None was seriously damaged because of the slow speed they were doing as they approached the junction. It seemed to be just front and back bumpers and headlamp glass. All the drivers were male and they were all talking to the policewoman, who was a very pretty girl. The comments went something like this:

'Don't worry, love, it'll mend.'

'It's only metal, duck, I'll get it fixed.'

'It could be worse, love; it's only a car after all.'

'Insurance will pay, duck, stop crying.'

Then someone gave her a cup of tea. I couldn't believe it, she'd obviously done something wrong but everyone was very forgiving. Had it been me that had caused the problems they'd have hanged me from the nearest lamp-post.

The men moved their cars and bits and pieces from the road and I went on traffic control. Fifteen minutes later it was back to normal and the traffic had eased off, so I asked her what had happened.

'I was doing fine and enjoying it. Some of the men in cars coming up Janson Street were blowing kisses at me and wolf-whistling and some of them had their fists up in the air and their arms were jigging up and down. I thought they must be waving, so I waved back. A car travelling from Sheffield thought I was telling him to stop and slammed his brakes on. The car behind ran into him and pushed him into the path of a car coming from Rotherham. The car behind him couldn't stop either – it was like being at the dodgems.' At that she burst into tears again.

My sides were splitting with trying not to laugh. She obviously didn't know that the signs made to her were, to put it mildly, suggestive and the thought of her waving back at the men who'd made them had me in stitches. If I'd told her what it meant and that her waving at them had caused an accident she would have been more upset than ever, so I left it alone.

There were very few policewomen in my early days but, apart from when you were in a pub fight, where you had to watch out for them before yourself, the lads and I had great respect for them. As far as we were concerned we were all working together for the same end and all part of the same team.

I loved working traffic control, especially at the bottom of Staniforth Road where it joined Attercliffe Road. The white coat and gloves were kept in the police box, along with the key to switch off the traffic lights. At rush hour the lights weren't able to cope with the volume of traffic. Normally you had time for a fag and a look at the rogues' gallery picture books which were kept in all police boxes in those days. At the appropriate time you switched the lights off and walked to the centre of the junction where all the traffic could be seen. There were three streams of traffic, each with two lanes, making six in all, and you had to really concentrate. There were no wolf whistles or kisses blown at me, and thankfully no arms with clenched fists either. You got to recognise the regular vehicle users, mainly bus and lorry drivers. They would beep and sometimes throw you a toffee as they drove past.

I got to know a regular bus driver on the 52 route, an old chap called Bob Newbold from Handsworth. I used to go for a pint with him from time to time. He was a grand fellow but whichever pub we went into in Sheffield or Derbyshire he would walk to the bar and not say a word.

'Usual, Bob?'

'Yes please,' he'd reply. His choice of drink was weird – a pint of Guinness and then a second empty pint pot and a fresh egg. He would crack the raw egg into the empty pot and then knock it back, followed by his pint of Guinness. I never saw him have two pints in the same place; he preferred instead to go to another pub where the process was repeated. Bob said it was good for you and he must have been right – he lived to a good age.

One time when I was directing traffic I noticed a stunning-looking girl with long blonde hair, wearing a cream and fawn checked suit. What a beauty, I thought; she must be a model. I thought she was looking at me but I couldn't be sure and I smiled at her just in case. Sure enough, the smile was returned. Wow! I nearly did what the policewoman had done – crash the cars. A minute later I had chance to look again but she was gone. Although I didn't know it then, that was my first sighting of Christine, my fantastic future wife.

Most of the tea-time traffic had now gone home and the roads were much quieter. I wondered how many people had driven past me on their various routes home; it must have been many thousands, judging by the hundreds and hundreds of vehicles that I had directed in the last hour and a half.

Snap-time was now calling. I could have eaten a flock bed I was so hungry but all I had were sardine sandwiches and two bananas. I loved bananas but had hated them when I was small. I remember my mum giving my sister and me our first banana and we got into trouble. Apparently they were on ration and hard to get hold of and Mum had queued for two hours to get them. Not having seen one before and not knowing they had to be peeled, we were eating the skin, which tasted horrible and put me off them for many years.

One afternoon a week we had to visit every pub on our respective beats with a sergeant. This was mainly to look for under-age drinkers or drinking after time, but as you had visited each one in turn, you knew where the local metal thieves were drinking and who their associates were. This was good information-gathering, especially later when we had police radios. You would spot a known criminal either in a pub or driving past you in a vehicle, radio the nick and pass the information to the Divisional Crime Collator, who would then log it for future reference. This could add to a pattern of their movements and, sometimes, destroy an alibi.

Most of the pubs, of which there were many, were fairly quiet, but some could be rough and it was these that we called at just after 10.40 pm, which was drinking-up time. Last orders were at 10.30 pm. I went into the first pub that evening with Sergeant Bowes. There were one or two beer-only pubs in the Attercliffe area in those days; they were usually frequented by men only and this was one of them.

Everything went quiet when we walked in and the dozen or so guys in there all had fullish pint pots of beer. Four lads in their thirties were sitting at a table. As we walked past, one of them stuck his leg out to trip me up. I saw it but it was too late and I sprawled across the next table, which was luck-ily devoid of glasses. Quick as a flash I was up, grabbing him by the lapels of his jacket and dragging him across the table. The other three were all laughing until they realised that their pint pots were now empty and on the floor.

'Put that poor man down, officer,' said Sergeant Bowes. He said it very slowly and very sternly and his voice was gruff. 'Now go and wait for me outside,' which I did.

A few minutes later he came out of the pub with Mr Tripper and his three mates. 'The four of you are now barred from these and other licensed premises in Attercliffe. You have assaulted one of my officers, who is a very strong young man and wishes to tear you apart, I'm sure. If you don't want that to happen I strongly advise you to apologise.'

'Sorry, sir, it won't happen again,' said Mr Tripper.

'Too right,' said the sergeant and very loudly shouted 'Boo!' in his face. The man nearly fainted. 'Now off you go home, little boy, and find some baby toys to play with – you're not big enough for anything else,' and the man was off.

The pub was now empty, apart from two full pints on the bar, one of which somehow found its way into my hand.

'Thank you, sergeant,' said the landlord. 'They've terrorised my customers for the last month – people daren't come in – it's cost me a load of custom. I didn't know how to stop them which is why I asked you to attend.'

'There are more ways to skin a cat than one, landlord. I don't think we'll see them again. Thanks for the beer. Goodnight.' And off we went.

The winter of 1962–3 was very bad and there was packed ice on the pavements for several months. I was working with Sergeant Bowes again and checking the pubs in the Darnall area. This time he'd left the King's Head on Poole Road until the last. Not because there would be anything wrong. It was a cracking pub used by cracking people. It's just that it was only two hundred yards from the police station where we finished at 11 pm.

It was a very cold night and most of the pubs were quiet. When you arrived at some of them you could sometimes see young people leaving and, obviously, other landlords we'd already visited had tipped the landlord off prior to our arrival. It didn't really matter, as prevention was better than cure.

One of the pubs on Darnall Terminus was the Wellington, run by Fred and Joan Lee. Fred was built like a bulldog, short and squat, and he was an ex-wrestler. They were a great couple and an excellent landlord and landlady. They stood no messing and kept a good house. I've only ever been called there twice and only once when Fred had it. Someone had phoned to say that there was a bit of bother there. Most unusual. Just as I got to the steps leading up to the front door it opened. Framed in the light was Fred, holding a chap's back collar in one hand and the back of his breeches with the other. In one movement Fred threw him and he landed on the pavement in front of me. I looked at him getting up – he was okay.

'I take it you're barred?' I said.

'Looks like it,' he answered, and off he went.

'Everything okay, Fred?' I asked.

'Aye, no trouble here, he seemed to want to leave in a

hurry so I obliged him. Knock on the back door if you want a pint later.'

We got to the King's Head on Poole Road and walked into a friendly atmosphere.

'Can I buy you a pint, Sergeant?' someone said.

'That's kind of you,' he said and put his hand out for the money. Having got it, he said to the customer, 'You know I can't drink on duty but that's my favourite charity,' and he pointed to a Dr Barnardo's collecting box on the bar. In went the money and everyone clapped, except the guy who'd thought he was being clever. The landlord was talking to Sergeant Bowes and off everyone went. A couple of minutes later we also left.

The pavements were very slippery that night and, as we gingerly walked towards the bus shelter, where all the people from the pub were waiting, Sergeant Bowes slipped and went down, grabbing my trousers and bringing me down with him. Because of the slope we crashed into the people at the bus stop and most of them went down as well, including the man who'd offered the pint. Nobody was hurt and we all got up laughing. A great way to finish a shift – or was it?

As I walked back to my digs I couldn't decide whether to go straight on or turn right towards Darnall Terminus and the Wellington, where Fred had offered me a pint at the back door. I sometimes called for a pint after day shift and it was not far from there to walk back to my digs.

The Wellington won over my conscience and I turned right to the pub. Once I had got past the English Bull Terriers in the yard, which Fred was famous for breeding, I then knocked on the back door. They were as friendly to me there as they were in the pub. Mucky dripping sandwiches were on the table in no time and, with a pint of bitter, it was a meal fit for a king. He used to call me Barnsley Bill and, after a few pints, he tried to talk like me. I had a lot of respect for Fred, he didn't suffer fools gladly and always spoke his mind. He didn't agree with burgling and, although he never grassed anyone up, he'd tell me who to keep an eye on.

About 1 am and several pints later I left the pub to walk the two hundred yards back to my digs. I must have wandered a bit because when I got in the clock said 1.40 am. I wasn't working again until 3 pm so it didn't matter and that seemed to me a far better way to finish a shift than going straight back to my digs.

Some time in the early sixties the government of the day decided to introduce a number of Police Mobile Columns. The country was in the throes of a Cold War with Russia and there was a very serious threat of nuclear war and terrorism. Apparently the Civil Defence movement was being disbanded and the Police Mobile Columns were to replace them.

The Mobile Columns were funded by the government and

they were deployed to various strategic parts of the country. Our particular one was stationed at Strensall army barracks, near York.

Policemen were chosen for their skills and, as I had previously been a blacksmith, I could forge things from iron, weld and use cutting gear. For this reason I was to be a search and rescue leader; other officers were cooks, drivers, wireless operators, motorcycle outriders, mechanics, storemen, map-readers and joiners.

In essence we were a self-contained and self-reliant unit operating mainly in the Yorkshire area. In the case of a nuclear strike we would be sent to the area of greatest devastation. As a youngster I lived not far away from a proper old gypsy encampment and along with them I became adept at catching and eating game birds, rabbits, fish and hedgehogs, which were a great delicacy. These extra skills were handy to have, but luckily for Great Britain we never got attacked and I never had to use them in a warfare situation.

As far as I can remember, each column consisted of about 120 officers plus a sergeant for every ten men, an inspector for every twenty men and a superintendent in overall charge. There were ten officers plus a sergeant to every Thames Trader lorry. Within the lorry, which looked a bit like the Group 4 prison vans of today, with blacked-out windows in the sides, were two long bench seats with a long table in between. There was no toilet and everyone had to use a communal bucket. The lorries were high up and we tended to be thrown about a lot. The same bucket was used by people who were travel-sick. You can imagine what it was like.

There were officers from all the geographical areas in Yorkshire on our column and our technical training took place in a long building in the old bus terminus near Wards Brewery at Snig Hill in Sheffield. The technical training relating to nuclear activity and fallout was very intense and the people who taught us were, I think, from scientific backgrounds. Most of the practical stuff was done at Strensall and we were helped by the army lads.

The first column that I went on after basic training was in 1965. We must have been quite a sight as we travelled in convoy through cities and open country, escorted by motorcycle outriders on army bikes. We drove non-stop with the outriders going ahead to ensure that we didn't have to stop or slow down for junctions or traffic lights. At first it was fun in the lorry and we would play cards to pass the time. But travelling conditions were rough – there was no ventilation, we didn't know where we were and travel sickness was a problem to us all. We were cooped up, sometimes for hours on end, and all you could hear was 'Bucket!' and someone else would be sick into it. Every time the bucket was full we had to somehow dispose of it en route because we didn't know how much further we had to travel. In the back door of the lorry was a small hatch which, when we looked through it, enabled us to tell whether we were in a town or open countryside. The lorry stank of sick and excrement and when we were in open country we had no option but to ditch the sick through the open hatch in the back door. Genuine mistakes were sometimes made and we got it wrong, and I'll leave you to imagine the scene when we did.

When we stopped to make camp it was all hands on deck. Latrines had to be dug, kitchens and tents set up. When we broke camp it was the reverse and anything edible or nasty had to be either burned or buried for hygienic reasons.

As a rescue leader it was my job to organise the retrieval of casualties from devastated buildings. For this purpose we would use large derelict buildings. I've had to improvise stretchers from old doors, pieces of wood lashed together with rope and, sometimes, metalwork. It was scary stuff lowering a colleague from a roof 100 feet off the ground. You had to get it right. We had a bad moment one day when we were near Richmond. A tractor pulled across the road in front of one of the motorcycle outriders – the poor man was killed instantly and left a wife and two small children.

Once we went to a coastal town somewhere up north where a simulated nuclear attack had taken place. Several buildings had been demolished and numerous bodies were lying on the beach below some pretty high cliffs. It was our job to recover the bodies and, after finding some old doors and ladders, we abseiled down the cliffs. Using the materials we found, we strapped the bodies to the doors and took them back up the cliff before the tide came in.

Being woken up at 1.30 am and getting the column ready for action was not an easy task but this was what used to happen when we were billeted at Strensall. The lads with the maps had been given map co-ordinates, presumably by the Home Office, and off we went on an unknown exercise. This was a freezing cold night late in the year and we ended up nearly home at Langset Reservoir, near Sheffield. Our instructions were to assume an imminent terrorist attack on the water supply to the Sheffield area. We had to map out all the inlets leading into the reservoir. It was fun in the dark until one or two of us fell in, but we survived.

The Mobile Columns weren't active for too long but, whilst they were, it was very interesting and a little-known aspect of some policemen's lives forty-five years ago. Luckily nothing happened and we are here to tell the tale. The world has moved on and now terrorism is world-wide. I fear for our grandchildren and their grandchildren and wonder where it will end.

CHAPTER NINE

UFOs: Am I Going Mad?

It was love at first sight. I was invited to a party in Darnall by a pal of mine and who was there but Christine, the girl I'd smiled at when working traffic control a few months before. Chatting to her, I discovered that she lived with her mum and dad, Mabel and Albert Mills, about 100 yards from where I was lodging. She was born in Attercliffe and lived there till she moved to Darnall when she was about eleven. She worked in the Publicity Department of Edgar Allen Engineering Ltd, on Shepcote Lane. At the time the chief accountant of Edgar Allen's was Mr Palin and in the summer months, in between university terms, his son Michael worked there. This was, of course, the Michael Palin who went on to become famous through the Monty Python television and film comedies and who travelled the world making documentaries.

Christine was very uncomplicated and easy to get on with. She was just as happy in the countryside haymaking or feeding the pigs and hens at Uncle Jack's farm as she was having a drink or going to the cinema. Later in our marriage, after producing three wonderful kids, Richard, Sally and Paul, she had an allotment and kept hens and is now a very proficient beekeeper. Strange really, she was a city girl who now is used to country ways, whilst I was a country lad who had to get used to city life. We are now in our fortieth year of marriage and I wouldn't swap her for the world; she might swap me though, so I'd better not ask.

I remember one day I'd been working Manor Top on foot patrol, ringing off duty at 11 pm. A quarter of an hour later saw me at Christine's house. Her mum had made me a sandwich, which was good considering the time of night I was calling to see her daughter. After that we took Sherry, her poodle, for a quick walk and a kiss and cuddle.

Christine lived near High Hazels Park, the entrance of which is in a valley formed by two opposing hills. As we were walking along hand in hand I suddenly saw two globular lights in the sky slowly coming towards us on the opposite hill, which we were facing. The best way I can describe them is that they were like the round balls on top of Belisha beacons. There were no beams of light coming from them and they were rhythmically and slowly pulsating. Every colour of the rainbow could be seen on them but there was no discernible noise whatsoever. We both stopped walking and I said to Christine, 'Can you see anything unusual?'

'Yes,' she said, 'two ball-like lights coming towards us. I was just going to ask the same question. What are they?'

While working nights out in the open I had seen shooting stars by the thousand, beams of light lasers shooting into the sky from the electric arc furnaces and all manner of things, but this had me stumped. At least I had corroboration – Christine had described to me exactly what I was seeing so I wasn't going mad. They, or maybe it, were travelling slowly and about twenty feet above the ground.

Christine was gripping my arm and hand by now. 'I'm frightened, let's go home. I don't like it,' she said. 'What is it?'

'I don't know. Just stay still.' At this point they seemed to alter course slightly, so that they were even more in line with where we were standing, and the pulsating lights were getting faster. I could feel the dog tugging and she was also barking like mad. Unbelievably, she broke her lead and ran back to the house barking and with her tail between her legs. I heard Mabel's voice as she opened the door. 'What's the matter, Sherry, have they left you?' Turning back now I could see that the lights were nearer and, in fact, looked as though they were perched on the ridge of the house roof ten feet from where we were standing. With that and given the height of an average house I would estimate that they were no more than thirty feet away from us. Christine was now shaking and I could see her trying not to look. They were pulsating faster now and emitting solid colours, all the colours of the rainbow. It was, to me, absolutely riveting and then, faster than a blink of an eye, there were four lights. We were spellbound or transfixed, I don't know which.

Everything that you have read we both agree on. It happened exactly as described, the only thing that we don't agree on is how long we watched them. Christine reckons three to four minutes, whilst I thought six to seven minutes. All we do know is that one second they were there and the next they were gone. Where to, who knows?

We both knew it wasn't a dream. It wasn't frightening to me and I didn't feel that we were in any danger. But whatever they or it was had certainly stopped to have a good look at us or it wouldn't have changed direction towards us. What the hell was it? We walked back the fifty or so yards to Christine's house and she quickly locked the door behind me. She was glad to be back indoors.

I ran back to my lodgings approximately 100 yards away. There was a fairly new policeman staying there as well by now. John was from London and had great difficulty understanding my Barnsley dialect. He was fast asleep and not too happy when I raked him out of bed. John had a car and I hadn't and I wanted to search for whatever I'd seen. I told him the story as he was getting dressed.

'What was it?' asked John

'That's the problem – I've no idea.'

'Where is it?'

'That's where you come in – I don't know.'

'What did they look like?'

'Balls, John. Balls!' And with that I dragged him to the car. We drove round the area for about half an hour but saw nothing. Logic told me that someone else must have seen it or them, but at 1 am there was no one knocking about to ask. I asked John to pull in near a pay-phone kiosk. I rang the night reporter on duty at the *Sheffield Star* offices.

'Have you had any reports of weird objects in the sky about an hour and a half ago?' I enquired.

'No, but can I have your details?'

'No way, pal, I'm a policeman. People will think I've gone mad.'

I told him the story and he was excited. 'Ring me back or call in, I'm going to ring the meteorological office at Bawtry. They may know something there. OK?'

After another twenty minutes of fruitless searching I'd had enough and spoke to John. 'I know that I saw what I saw but just don't know what it was. Let's call in at the *Star* office and see if they have turned anything up.'

The rear of the *Star* offices was a hive of activity. Lorries were unloading massive rolls of paper, men stacking and moving newspapers by the thousand, all needing to be put in the small delivery vans waiting to distribute the *Morning Telegraph* to the shops.

One of the men obliged us by phoning the night reporter. 'Are you the policeman who rang up a while ago?' he shouted to me.

'Yes.'

'He wants you upstairs urgently – he's got something.'

When we got to the large upstairs office you could hear the phones ringing and a chap, obviously the reporter, was trying to answer them. He turned to us after putting the phone down.

'Nothing from the met office, but since you phoned me seven different people have rung up from across the city – that last one was from Dore Village. Sometimes two, sometimes four lights and just like you described.'

The phone rang again and when he answered it he mouthed, 'another' and put his thumb up in the air. By the time we left there were about twelve sightings and I was later informed that there were twenty-eight sightings in total, including one from a man who was at the top of High Hazels Park at the same time as we were at the bottom. He described exactly what we had seen. The object or objects had gone over him and down the park where he saw them change from two to four. They seemed to be on the roof of a house and then they just disappeared. At least I knew I wasn't going mad. With that we went home to bed at about 3 am.

'Martyn! Get up! Get up now, you are wanted.' It was Mrs Proctor shouting from downstairs.

'I've only just got to bed and don't want to get up yet,' I yelled.

'Get up and get up now, the police inspector wants to see you.'

I could see from my alarm clock that it was 8.30 am. I wondered what he could want to see me for, I hadn't done anything wrong.

I came downstairs and there was the inspector. 'Yes, sir?' I said.

'Best uniform, best boots and white gloves, the superintendent wants to see you.' I only had one pair of boots, I couldn't afford another pair, so I had to wear them. This was serious stuff – what the hell had I done wrong? To see an inspector was bad enough but a superintendent was like going to deal with the man from heaven – or hell.

I was driven to the police station at Whitworth Lane and the inspector told me that when I was asked to enter the superintendent's office I was to march to the front of his desk and salute.

The inspector knocked on the door and was told to enter. 'PC 656 Johnson to see you, sir.'

'Send him in.'

As I marched into the office and saluted I was wishing my trousers were brown and not blue.

'Yes, sir.'

'I understand that you saw something unusual just after midnight last night?'

'Yes, sir.'

'Did you report it?'

'No, sir.'

'Why not?'

'I didn't know what it was to report, sir, or that it was important to do so.'

At this point he indicated two men sitting to his left. They were both wearing trilby hats and cream trench coats fastened with belts, the sort of clothes that spies wore on television.

'These two gentlemen have travelled up from London during the night and are members of a government investigation department. They want to interview you, okay?

'Don't worry, you're not in trouble. Feel free to use my office,' and with that the superintendent left.

I was asked to sit down and to relate the night's events, which I did. I was then asked to repeat the story twice more. I would imagine that they were looking for inconsistency and they were right to.

'Sorry, I forgot to mention the dog. I'm sure it's nothing.'

I told them the story of the dog being frightened and they were surprisingly interested and added it to their already copious notes.

'Is there any significance with the dog?' I asked.

'Yes, you heard no noise, but animals can hear noises that we can't. It must have heard something which made it bark when the object got nearer – probably ultrasonic sound.'

They asked for Christine's details and any other witnesses. I explained that they'd have to contact the *Star* for those. By this time I was intrigued. How did they know what had happened so quickly and what was it that had triggered their departure from London in the early hours? It was a good three-hour journey in those days. They obviously knew something that I didn't.

The next day I was taken to a courtroom in Sheffield. There were the two government men, myself and another man who I assumed to be a magistrate, because I had to swear on oath not to relate the story for twenty-five years. I thought this a bit weird as it was in the newspapers and I think the heading in the *Star* was 'Bright Lights in Sky'. One or two more reports had come in apparently, one from Derbyshire, one from Congleton in Cheshire and sightings on the Cheshire coast, and all on the same night. There was also a report from a woman who had seen them over Rotherham, after she had finished work at RAF Bawtry. I'd kept an open mind on what I'd seen but it was certainly weird and the route across country appeared very erratic. I'd earlier taken the men to the scene and they seemed very interested. They asked me whether or not the dog was looking at the objects when she was barking but I couldn't answer that as Christine and I were watching the lights, not the dog.

The men stayed for three days. I assumed that they were seeing witnesses, but the funny thing to me was that they never interviewed Christine. However, they did interview the man at the top of the park who'd seen what we saw but from the opposite direction. By chance I was in the station mess room just as they were about to leave for London and I was curious.

'Do you mind telling me what I have seen?' They looked at each other, shrugged their shoulders and smiled and these words are indelibly stamped on my brain today, some forty-two years after the event: 'What you have seen is an unknown flying object or UFO. Some people call them spaceships, and if the people of the world knew how many genuine sightings like your own there were there would be a world panic. That is without doubt what you have seen.' At that point they said cheerio and went.

I received several letters addressed to me at the police station from UFO societies, quite a lot from overseas, asking for information on the sighting. I didn't reply to any of them, I'd been sworn to secrecy.

I was nicknamed 'UFO' by the lads for ages but ever since

that night and for over forty years now I have a periodic dream about being in a spacecraft and looking through a large window. In the darkness beyond are two flotillas of flying objects of funny shapes. One lot is crimson red, the other is a beautiful blue colour. That is it, nothing else. What did it mean? If anything? Who knows, I don't. Maybe I'm mad after all. Beam me up, Scotty!*

*Since writing the above, it has been established that this sighting took place on Tuesday 23 June 1968. I would like to thank Paul Licence of the Sheffield *Star* for his help; and also Mick Butcher of the same newspaper, for his diligence in ascertaining the information.

This chapter is dedicated to Craig Horner.

Editor's note:
The Ministry of Defence closed its UFO Investigation Unit in November 2009. The MoD justified its decision to axe the X-*Files*-style unit by saying there was no 'defence value' in investigating sightings. However, past files on UFOs will continue to be released for public scrutiny by the National Archives.

CHAPTER TEN

Here, Pussy, Pussy

W orking the night shift on a foot beat sounds boring to some people. I can honestly say that I've never been bored in my life. If you've ears to listen with, eyes to see with and a brain to think with (no disrespect to anyone who hasn't got those faculties, you have my sympathy), you should never be bored.

Between 11 pm and 3 am is usually quite busy working a beat but after that it can drag a bit, mainly through tiredness. I was on No. 14 beat at Tinsley. This beat is usually worked on a push-bike but my pink and yellow one had been 'stolen' a few weeks before so I was on foot. It suited me better that way but it was a fair distance between points, so I would have to walk quickly. At the end of Coleridge Road was the Salutation pub and I was just passing when I saw a ginger tomcat on the pavement. 'Here, puss, puss,' I called and he came to me and slithered round my legs. I picked him up and rushed back to the terraced houses opposite the nick. Mrs Smith, a lovely old lady, lived there alone and, according to the duty sergeant, her pet ginger tom had gone missing earlier in the day. We all liked her and she had told the sergeant that she had left the cellar grate unlocked and if we found him, we should pop him in the cellar. I did just that and managed to make my next point at the end of Broughton Lane in time. From there I walked down Attercliffe Common, checking the shops for break-ins as I went.

My next point was Tinsley police box, which was situated on the bridge overlooking the canal. Although bitterly cold, it was a beautiful night. The moon was full and I could see from the bridge that it lit up the Plumpers public house and Ron's Transport Café at the side of the canal. I rang in from the police box for two reasons. First, to tell the sergeant that I was okay and secondly in the hope that he wouldn't look for me after my next-but-one point because I was going to purposely miss it out.

I almost ran to my next point, the city boundary at Templeborough, where it joined Rotherham. There were several steelworks built here, unfortunately on top of a Roman fort. As a country lad the works were a novelty and I was fascinated by the noise, the light and the heat. The pavement was about an inch thick with residual ash from the furnaces and, when you breathed in, it clogged up your mouth. No wonder there were no houses around. Looking through the iron railings allowed you to see heavy locomotives pulling flat trailers. They were laden with enormous steel ingots, glowing white hot with sparks flying off them as the cold air made contact. They were maybe fifty yards from where I was standing and the heat and the smell that they gave off was amazing.

With a bit of luck I would witness one of the finest free shows on earth. The enormous electric furnace stood approximately forty to fifty feet high or possibly higher and had been filled with loads of scrap steel or iron (I did not know which, but I think iron). I was the only spectator – no other audience for the incredible display I was hoping to see.

A few minutes later I heard a low deep hum. I was thinking, 'This is it, get ready,' whilst looking through the railings and across the darkness to the steelworks. I could see two huge electrodes glowing red with heat and slowly being lowered into the furnace below. As they made contact with the raw materials the noise was deafening and huge showers of sparks were flying everywhere. It looked brilliant. There was no escape for the scrap metal; no matter which way it twisted and turned it couldn't get away – the monster was the electrodes and the metal their prey. Eventually the noise and sparks stopped, the electrodes had won and the scrap was now a white-hot liquid, awaiting the next event. The electrodes were slowly withdrawn, glowing white like the steel. Men were now rushing up and down along the gantries getting ready to pour the molten metal. The size of the furnace made them look tiny.

After a while, Act Two began with a hissing noise and then, through the holes in the roof of the building, rays of light shot high into the sky. I got glimpses of white-hot liquid metal snaking down some sort of chute and making its way into what I assumed were the moulds for the ingots. The pyrotechnic show was now over. I'm glad I did not miss it. A couple of hundred yards away was the Temple pub and its doors would open at 6 am, by special licence, to allow the men on night shift to take in much-needed liquid to replace the sweat they had lost whilst working. Theirs was a dangerous job. Many a poor chap lost his life or was maimed whilst working in the steelworks. Just like the miners they worked hard and, between them, did more than their fair share to justify our nation being called Great Britain.

I made my way back to the nick and wolfed down my potted-meat sandwiches and a bag of crisps (the ones with the little blue bag of salt in them). The sergeant hadn't missed me, so I was in the clear. A quick game of table tennis in the parade room and I was out on the beat again.

The rest of the night was uneventful but not boring, and I was back at the nick for 6.55 am, ready to sign off at 7 am.

I was exhausted with all the walking – no wonder it was a push-bike beat.

There were five of us signing off when the duty sergeant came into the parade room. With him, of all people, was Mrs Smith from across the road, lovingly stroking her ginger tom-cat. The look on her face was all the reward I needed for racing to her house earlier in the night with her pet.

'Mrs Smith would like to thank whoever found her cat – who was it?' All five of us said, 'Me, Sergeant,' at the same time, and looked at each other in amazement. I suppose there must have been dozens of ginger cats living within a couple of hundred yards of the nick and many hundreds of houses. We had each found a cat we assumed was hers and genuinely done our good deed. She had been woken by the cats' meow-ing and, when she opened the cellar door, five cats shot into the kitchen. One was hers so she let the others out to make their own way home. Everyone was laughing now and I went back to my digs tired but happy.

When I got back to the digs Mrs Proctor was, as usual, up and washing clothes. In the living room was her son George, or Jud as most people called him. Jud, I suppose, would have been in his forties then and he was a bit of a character. He would do anything for anyone, even though he was rather a rough diamond. He worked a night shift somewhere and he and his wife also ran a small shop in Hillsborough. He used to call and see his mum on his way from work and always brought her something, such as tins of biscuits, punnets of strawberries, sultanas or sugar. You name it, he brought it.

'Just done, duck, have you?' Jud asked me.

'Yes, Jud, but it's been a bit quiet apart from the cat incident.' I told him and his mum the story about the cats and they laughed their heads off.

'It's a good job there were only five of you and not twenty-five,' said Jud and we all laughed again at the thought of twenty-five cats in one cellar.

'C'mon, I'll take you for your breakfast if you've nothing to do.'

'Where are you going?' I asked.

'Don't you worry about that, young 'un – put your civvy jacket on and, if anybody says anything to you, don't let on you're a copper, okay?'

I'd already got my jacket on and we were off. Anything different was a change for me and I could sleep later.

Jud had an old Bedford van and he headed towards the city, which I still didn't know very well then. The only bit I recognised was the old West Bar police station and the stables for the police horses. Later on they moved up to Tapton Road. He turned down a small cobbled street somewhere near there and pulled up in a narrow lane behind an oldish building. There was a small wooden door set within two large wooden gates and Jud knocked on it. When it opened a chap in a blood-soiled white smock and white hat looked out to his left and right and then passed out some cardboard boxes which were put in the back of the van. At the same time I heard Jud say, 'Here, duck, that's that fiver I owe you,' and off we drove. It was now 8 am and I was starving.

'Where are we going now?' I asked Jud.

'I've just got to drop some stuff off at the market. Won't be long.'

The market turned out to be the Sheffield wholesale market. It was a huge complex that I'd never been to before, but all that would later change. We arrived there at about 8.30 am and drove past the security office and turned left to the wholesale fish market. The place was alive with people chucking boxes of fish into vans from the outside fish docks. We were driving slowly now, Jud pipped and a guy on the fish dock waved and indicated for Jud to reverse up, which he did. Jud jumped out of the van and took two boxes out of the back of the vehicle and put them onto the fish dock. I was to learn later that our boxes contained full hams and ham hocks. Blimey, before we arrived at the market there must have been enough pork in our van to feed a small village. Three large boxes of fish were then thrown into the back of our vehicle, along with a box of fresh crabs.

From there we went to the fresh vegetable side of the market. Out of the back of the van Jud took one more of our boxes containing the ham hocks and a couple of large pieces of fish, and a furtive-looking guy chucked potatoes, cabbages, tomatoes, celery, apples and oranges into the back of the van and accepted our two boxes.

Next were the flower stalls, where some of our stuff was removed only to be replaced by loads of fresh flowers.

'I'll bet you're ready for your breakfast,' said Jud, and drove us to a building containing a café. In we went with a couple of parcels of fish and two crabs, which were given to the ladies behind the counter.

'Usual, George?' asked one.

'Please, duck, and one for my mate, he's on leave from the RAF,' he said, pointing to my blue shirt.

'How long have they had truncheons in the RAF, George?'

Too late, I realised that the leather truncheon strap was hanging from its pocket and open to view below my jacket.

'He's just driven from RAF Finningley. He's on the security side there, and hasn't had chance to change,' was the explanation.

With that the other woman brought two of the biggest breakfasts that I'd ever seen to the table, along with two pint pots of tea. There were four sausages, two eggs, four rashers of bacon, fried bread, mushrooms, tomatoes, beans and black pudding, followed by toast. In those days I could eat but even though I was ready for it, I struggled a bit.

We got back to the van and Jud told me to leave my door open. One of the women arrived and plonked ten dozen eggs on four trays on my knee and about ten packs of Wall's bacon in the well of the car.

'Cheerio and thanks for the breakfast, duck,' said Jud.

'Thanks for the fish and crabs, George, see you next week.'

On the way back to his shop we chatted about all sorts including how hard a life his mum had had bringing up ten children, plus the two that were adopted. He told me that if she stopped looking after people she'd die, that's why she had three lodgers; she didn't need the money from it but the two other lodgers and I helped to keep her going. There was a tear in his eye when he quietly said, 'Thanks.'

Back at the shop I helped him unload the van. I'd been sat in the front before we went into the café so I didn't see what was in the back and I couldn't believe how much stuff was inside. On the way back to his mum's I asked what I owed him for breakfast.

'It was part of the deal, duck,' he replied.

'What deal?' I naively asked him.

'My van full of stuff and breakfast cost me £5. It's called commercial enterprise.' He dropped me off with some eggs and bacon to give to his mum along with a crab for my dinner. At that age and with less than a year's service I couldn't reckon up what commercial enterprise meant. It sounded legal but, on the other hand, how could you get all that for £5?

A few weeks after this he asked if I'd help him lift some

tables from his shop. He picked me up in his van and we went to his shop where I helped him to arrange the tables in the short cobbled street. After they were set up they were loaded with mountains of food and pop and chairs were put around them.

It was a sunny Sunday afternoon and all the old people and kids from the locality were being treated to a slap-up meal; and all courtesy of Jud. They had party hats and streamers and an old gramophone was playing records by Bill Haley and a fairly new group called The Beatles. The women and kids were bopping away and having a lovely time. I left to catch the bus back to The Cliffe to start afternoons at 3 pm. The next morning I went to help him tidy up and Jud told me there had been about sixty people there the day before. He went on to say that some of the women were widows and some of the kids' dads had been killed in the works or were unable to work because of serious injuries they'd suffered.

'Once a year they go on a club trip to Cleethorpes or Mablethorpe and once a year I put a do on for them, that's all they get. They are poor people and are my customers so I try to look after them as best I can.'

Over the years I was to deal with 'jack the lads', likeable rogues, criminals, rapists, gangsters and murderers. Jud was none of these; he was a hard-working guy who wouldn't hurt a soul and his mum used to say, 'Our George will never have any money, he puts others first, but that's how I brought them all up so I can't complain.' He was always laughing and joking and helping other people worse off than himself. This, in my book, is as it should be. I adopted one of his sayings, which was 'No one is better than you and no one is worse than you.'

CHAPTER ELEVEN

Wakey, Wakey

It had been perhaps three months since I last worked the motorcycle beat at Firth Park and that was on a night shift.

On this occasion I was on the day shift, starting at 7 am at The Cliffe where I picked up the bike. It was a lovely Sunday morning and very few people were knocking about. I rode down to Fir Vale where I turned right towards Firth Park. Part of all policemen's duties in those days was to check that the public clocks were working correctly and, if not, inform the city estates department. There were only two in our division – Darnall church clock and the one that I was about to pass, Firth Park Tower. The clock was in good working order and it reminded me of my last night shift up here.

It had been a fairly quiet night and the two foot-beat

bobbies and myself met together at the sub-station near the top of Stubbin Lane for our snap and a quick game of cards before rejoining our respective beats. All was quiet until about 5.30 am when the motorcycle radio sounded in my ear. 'PC John Colley has not been seen by the sergeant for forty minutes and has missed his last two points – request urgent search of his area.'

For the next twenty minutes or so I checked his beat without success and was worried that something was wrong with my mate. Where was he? Was he okay? I had to find him. I wonder, I wonder if ... It's surprising what crosses your mind. I'd worked with John before so I rode to a place just on the edge of his beat where there was a bus shelter. As I approached it I could see twelve to fifteen men standing there, waiting for the arrival of a bus to take them to work. They didn't seem to be talking to each other, which I thought was odd because they must meet every morning at the same time.

I got off the motorbike and wished them good morning and they answered very quietly and in a hushed tone. The next thing I heard was an almighty snore and, brushing past two of the men, I saw my mate John. At least he was alive. He was lying at full stretch on the bus shelter seat, covered up with his cape and snoring like a pig. His helmet and a small alarm clock were near his head. What a sight. At this time the bus arrived to pick up the men and as they were getting on board they whispered to me, 'He looked so peaceful, we daren't wake him up,' and 'Even my missis can't snore like that'; and they were all laughing after they got on the bus.

'John, John, wake up!' I shouted, and up he shot, not knowing where he was. When I told him why I was there he said, 'That bloody alarm clock's useless.' I radioed in to say that he was safe but had sprained his ankle whilst in pursuit of someone, which they accepted, and I gave him a ride back to the nearest sub-station.

That had been about three months before but it still made me laugh when I thought about it.

That morning it was about 7.15 am when I arrived at the sub-station and the phone was ringing inside. I hoped it wasn't a job, as I'd not yet had breakfast – I was hoping to get one down the road at the staff canteen in the Northern General Hospital. It was the duty sergeant back at Attercliffe: 'I know it's not your area but a train driver thinks he's seen the remains of a body on the railway line, somewhere on Woolley Wood Road, near Ecclesfield. A new sergeant and a PC have gone to look. Can you go and assist with the search?'

'That's put paid to breakfast for a while,' I thought to myself, as I rode to join the search.

About half a mile before the location of the incident, and

near the Ecclesfield boundary, I saw a saloon car parked in a lay-by, only about twenty-five yards from the railway line, which ran on top of a rise near to me. I pulled in to check out the car; its two front windows were wide open. My immediate thoughts were that we could be dealing with a suicide and that I'd found the person's car, especially when I spotted the keys in the ignition and realised the bonnet of the car was hot – it hadn't been there long. I looked in the car for a suicide note but couldn't see one. I radioed in to the office to give the vehicle details and my location; then asked if the sergeant had found anything yet.

'Not yet, I think he's about a quarter of a mile down the track from you,' they replied.

'I think it is probably a suicide,' and I told them why. 'I'll get to the line and look for the sergeant.'

I went through a wooded thicket and, as I was climbing the bank, I was looking to my right for the sergeant. Sure enough I could see him and shouted, 'Anything?' and I saw him shake his head. Where I'd arrived there was a brick bridge where the line crossed a culvert. I lit a fag while waiting for the sergeant and leaned on the wall of the small bridge.

Looking down and across the line I saw it, or should I say what was left of it: bits of skull and brain tissue, top teeth attached to part of a face, and looking to my right I could see, at the side of the track, an arm and further on still a leg.

I called the sergeant over and we inspected the scene, trying not to be sick. From the outset it was obvious that the initial impact was fairly high up on the bridge wall as most of the remains of the head were close by. Most railway suicides either jumped in front of the train or lay down on the track in front of it. Had that happened in this instance, the driver of the train would have known and obviously reported it. If the victim had been on the train and jumped out he would more than likely have gone over the top of the bridge because of the height of the train. Alarm bells were ringing big time – both our thoughts were moving from suicide to murder.

About fifteen minutes after our arrival we radioed back to Attercliffe and told them what was what. We asked for the Criminal Investigation Department to attend and also the railway police, and for the line to be shut down. Shortly after this everyone arrived, including the police photographer, the police surgeon, Professor Alan Usher, and the head of CID.

At this time I was on the sidelines and looking on. After lots of discussions, photographs and measurements someone asked who had found the body and the sergeant pointed to me. The head of the CID, Superintendent Chambers, said, 'Right, son, you go to the mortuary with Professor Usher and assist him. Tomorrow come to work in civvies, you are the exhibits officer in this case.'

Unfortunately there wasn't much of the body left to do a post-mortem on, and I won't go into more details here. By the time we were done it was 1 pm and Professor Usher could see I was a bit groggy. 'When did you last eat?' he asked.

'About 8 pm last night, sir,' I replied.

'Go outside to my car and fetch my jacket please.' I did as I was told. 'You've had a rough and unpleasant day and you haven't eaten, put this jacket on and follow me.' I hadn't a clue where we were going as we walked down Nursery Street, and then he walked into the Manchester Hotel and told me to sit down. He pointed to a table. He handed me a double whisky and then two meals were placed in front of us. 'I know you don't feel like eating after what you've seen but you'll feel a lot better afterwards,' and he was right, I did. What a guy. I couldn't believe that someone as important as him would bother with someone like me. What a gentleman he was – no wonder everyone who knew him held him in such high esteem.

Back at the scene I gave the superintendent Professor Usher's report and, after reading it, he said, 'Thank you, go and sign off and I'll see you at nine in the morning. There's nothing more you can do here today.'

The case was now in the hands of the CID and, apparently, their inquiries had already begun. I went back to the motorbike and suddenly remembered the car with the keys in the ignition. The vehicle had now gone. It couldn't have belonged to the body on the line or it would still be there. I made a note to check it out later. It was Sunday anyway and the Driver and Vehicle Licensing Authority wouldn't be open until 9 am on Monday. There were no police computers in those days so it would have to wait. I signed off and went home. It was only about ten hours since I had found the body but it felt like a week. I was shattered and went to bed early.

The next morning I found that an incident room had been set up at the station, comprising the detectives on the job, a secretary to collate information, a typist and me. At 9 am the superintendent brought us up to date at a briefing.

The body was that of a thirty-nine-year-old man who lived in Sheffield and had been identified by his clothing and his personal effects, which were found scattered at the scene. He had been to a seminar in Leeds and should have been back in Sheffield at about 10.30 pm – but he never arrived. His worried wife reported him missing on the Sunday morning. Inquiries were ongoing to trace the passengers on his train and I was asked to check out the car with the keys left in it. It hadn't been reported stolen so why was it there?

Not being part of the investigating team and not having many exhibits to record, I contacted the DVLA at Swansea and got the car owner's details. Then I went to the house, which was about a mile from the scene. It was about 2.30 pm and I saw that the bedroom curtains were closed and thought that perhaps the driver was a night-shift worker. I recognised the car in the drive. I knocked on the door and it was opened by a man who looked as though he had just woken up. I was in civvies so he didn't know who I was until I showed him my warrant card, at which point he nearly fainted. 'Come in,' he stuttered. 'The wife's at work.'

I told him the reason for my visit and asked him why his car was in the lay-by with open windows and the keys in the ignition. After a long pause he started to speak.

'I'm a night foreman in the steelworks and one of the girls in the canteen has been chatting me up for weeks. I finished work at 7 am on Sunday morning and I said I'd give her a lift home.'

'What happened then?' I asked.

'She told me to pull into that lay-by where you saw it. She jumped out of the car and ran to the edge of those trees and was laughing as she took all her clothes off and beckoned me to her. That's where we were when we saw you arrive and we hid until you went onto the bridge. Please don't tell the wife, she'll kill me.'

'Tell her to wait a week before she kills you, we're busy at the moment.' I didn't enlighten him about what I meant, and after telling him to take his morning exercise elsewhere, I was off. I checked his story with the girl later and it was correct.

The day after this I took some of the dead man's clothes to the forensic laboratory in Harrogate. This was the nearest one in those days, and when I got back the CID chaps had made an arrest as a result of a tip-off. They were also looking for someone else. As exhibits officer I was only on the fringe of things but I was told that there had been an argument on the train which resulted in a fight. Our man was beaten up in the corridor and, as he lay on the floor, one man opened the train door and callously pushed him out. The body bounced back onto the track and, during the night, other trains had hit it in the darkness.

A couple of days later I was told that the other guy had been arrested and, after interview, had been taken to Armley Jail in Leeds to await trial. I was asked to go up there to pick up his boots and take them to the forensic laboratory in Harrogate.

The M1 to Leeds hadn't been open long and it was very quiet. For company I took my old neighbour Harry – he was a grumpy old man but a cracking crib partner. I was once walking with him into the Masons' Arms at Thorpe Hesley when two girls I knew from Darnall were just leaving. We said hello and later I told Harry, who was then about seventy-five years old, that they were both lesbians. I was having a bit of fun, I suppose; curious to know what the old chap's reaction would be. He came out with one of his infamous replies. Looking at me with a straight face he said,

'Don't talk bloody daft, man. How can they be lesbians? They are both women!' I nearly bust a gut with laughing and then he muttered under his breath, 'I've always wondered what that word meant. Don't tell anybody that I didn't know, will you?'

Armley Jail was a very old and austere-looking building. I hadn't been there before. In we went and after showing my warrant card I explained why I was there . A warder came to fetch me; for obvious reasons security was tight. My eyes were everywhere as doors were unlocked and then shut and locked behind us again. I'd meant to leave Harry at reception and explained that to the warder. 'No problem – just sit in there, we'll not be long.' He pointed to a door which had a notice on it that said Interview Room. In Harry popped and the warder closed the door. A few minutes later I picked up the boots, which were in a sealed plastic bag. I was shown back to the reception by another warder and then off I went to take the boots to the lab in Harrogate. I'd just left the lab and was near Pannal Ash Police College when I suddenly thought of poor Harry. I'd left him in jail!

By the time I got back I'd been gone an hour and a half. Luckily for me he'd banged on the door of what he thought was a cell and the first warden realised what had happened and took him to reception. He had just been given a cup of tea when I arrived. Harry wasn't happy. 'You bloody thing you, leaving me in that condemned cell. How would you like

it, spending the rest of your life in there? I thought I would be.'
I could see the funny side of it but daren't laugh and I was full
of apologies, which made no difference whatsoever to poor
old Harry. He was still cursing me when we got to Dodworth
on the M1, where the road goes steeply downhill. I had to
appease him somehow. 'Have you ever done 100 mph, Harry?'

'Only racing cars can do that,' he said, grudgingly.

Going down the incline, I touched 100 mph for a second
or two. I glanced at him and he was waving to everyone we
passed and laughing his head off. It was good to laugh again,
something I'd not done for about a week. But being involved
with a job like that was, of course, no laughing matter.

Some time later both men pleaded guilty to murder at
Sheffield Assize Court and, as far as I can recall, were each
given twelve years. If they got remission for good behaviour
they would probably do eight. It didn't sit right with me
then, and it doesn't today. A poor woman had lost her husband and two young children were fatherless.

CHAPTER TWELVE

Live and Learn

I joined the police force because all I ever wanted was to be on the beat, which in those days was all there was anyway. I wanted to be a copper or bobby, working with people, not against them – apart from, of course, criminals. Being a sergeant, a detective or traffic officer held no interest for me whatsoever. I was more than happy being your ordinary everyday Dixon of Dock Green or PC Plod. I was and still am a people person; even in the city suburbs, where many thousands lived, you got to know the people and they got to know you.

On this particular morning shift I had with me a new policeman to show round and he was full of it. We walked down to Attercliffe Baths corner and watched the early morning traffic for a while.

'How many motorists will you report today?' he asked.

'None,' I replied, 'unless they knock me down.'

'Will we catch a TWOC?' (Taken Without Owner's Consent – or a stolen vehicle).

'I doubt it at this time of day.'

'Will it be two or three years before I become a sergeant? I got seven GCEs at grammar school and was top in all my exams at the Training School.' All of this was in the first thirty minutes of meeting him and we had another seven-and-a-half hours to go. Why they had put this pretentious, bumptious, arrogant person with me I didn't know. I've never suffered fools gladly and always talked John Bull. Maybe *that* was why they put him with me, I thought. This little boy needed some serious de-education and a bit of help and guidance as well.

'Come on, we've got work to do, it's nearly 8 am.'

'Anything exciting?' he asked.

'We'll see,' I said, as we walked up The Cliffe. We walked to Clare's Café – owned and run not by Clare but by Renee and Audrey. They were two nice and hard-working ladies. It was chock-a-block with people from the steelworks and other allied businesses. They were all queuing out of the front door. The local workers only had short snap-times and all wanted serving quickly. Up the two recently scoured steps we went, through the back door and into the kitchen where Renee was cooking as fast as she could.

'Morning, Martyn, I'm glad to see you,' and with that I grabbed four or five sliced loaves and went to the toasting machine in the corner. Lifting the lid I put in four slices which was all it would take and at the same time passed PC Pretentious a pack of butter and a knife. 'When this toast is done, butter it and put it on the table near Renee.' His face was a picture.

About an hour later the rush was over and empty bread wrappers were everywhere, we'd earned our breakfast and a pot of tea and after a quick chat with the scrap lads in the front we were on our way again, having been thanked by Renee and Audrey. Nearly all the lads used the café and some of the sergeants as well.

We meandered back onto The Cliffe and a little old lady stopped us.

'Excuse me, but do you know my grandson? He's a policeman like you.'

'What's his name, love?'

'John—. I've seen a picture of him in uniform. I'm so proud.'

'I'm sorry, love, I can't think that I know him. Does he work in Attercliffe?'

'No, London. He's just joined.'

'Ha, yes. I think I've met him. Is he tall?'

'Yes, that's him. I'm glad you know him.'

'Say hello from Martyn when you next see him.'

'I haven't seen him since he was eight. They don't have time to come, but they write to me.'

Over the years I would see the old lady quite a lot, and she'd fill me in with the latest news such as his engagement, marriage and children. She was lovely and needed to talk to someone who she thought knew him. I must have known her for eight or nine years but she still hadn't seen him. Had that been my grandma I'd have wrapped her up in cotton wool. She was a little sweetheart. When I didn't see her any more I realised that she must have died, and I was mad with myself for not asking where her grandson lived, in the hope that I could have got him up to see her. What a shame I didn't.

The main Attercliffe road was quiet now and, as we got near to Sam Kitter's dress shop at the end of Vicarage Road, a lady stopped us.

'I need you to come and see what we have just found at the side of the clinic.' The clinic was near the end of Vicarage Road and just past the old Adelphi Cinema, which was frequented by young and old at that time. 'I've just found a bomb at the side of the clinic.' She was obviously shaken up and sounded very nervous.

The Attercliffe area and its many scrapyards were full of old munitions from the Second World War. The police station was always getting calls about kids playing with them or taking them to school and the main source of supply was

Tommy Ward's scrapyard at Tinsley. It wasn't the scrapyard owner's fault, it was in a child's nature to scrim over the wall and play with the remnants of World War Two which had been sent to the scrapyard for disposal. They didn't realise the danger they were in. These incidents happened so often that a brick-built shelter, full of sandbags, was built in the side yard of the nick to house the items until they were collected by the bomb disposal lads from York.

We went to investigate what the lady had found near the clinic and it turned out to be a Second World War hand grenade with its pin intact – they are perfectly safe if the pin is left in situ. After borrowing a bucket I filled it with sand and put the grenade in the middle. I collected PC Pretentious, who was standing behind a wall, and set off to walk the quarter mile to the police station. We were about to cross Attercliffe Road when we heard a squeal of brakes. A black Rolls-Royce was stationary at the zebra crossing. The driver, in chauffeur uniform and with a smile on his face, had anticipated that we were going to cross and was obviously showing off his driving skills to his passenger. But as we turned onto the crossing there was an almighty bang and an old Wards Brewery wagon, full of casks of beer, slammed into the back of the Roller and shunted him down the road a few yards. The chauffeur's smug smile was gone and he and the driver of the wagon were now arguing as to whose fault it was. Out got the passenger, a portly man in a pin-striped suit, who spoke very posh.

'Sort this out. I'm in a hurry,' he said to me, and at the same time looked at me as if I was something on his shoe. Pretentious number two, I thought, and that is one too many for me. I wanted to polish my right boot on the seat of his trousers but resisted the temptation. Without even a 'sir', I said, 'It is a non-injury accident and can be reported at any police station.' At the same time I proffered him the bucket, saying, 'Inside that bucket is a live bomb that could go off at any time. If you hold the bucket for me I'll take a few details.'

'Er, no, we'll report it later,' and he ran behind the brewery wagon and hid.

When we got round the corner, even PC Pretentious joined me in a good laugh and asked, 'Where are we going to put the grenade?'

'I know where I'd like to have put it,' I replied.

'Me too,' he said, and laughed. We got back to the station and sang to the sergeant, 'There's a bomb in my bucket, dear sergeant, dear sergeant, there's a bomb in my bucket, dear sergeant – a bomb.'

After snap-time we walked back up The Cliffe and I had a chat with Ernest, a fruit and vegetable barrow boy, who pitched up at the bottom of Shortridge Street. He was a great guy and we've swapped many a good joke together. From there we went down Effingham Road and near to where Lovetot Road joins it. I showed PC Pretentious the plaque set in the red-brick wall commemorating the lives of nine men, ten women and ten children who lost their lives to a German bomb on 26 September 1916. I always muttered a little prayer of respect every time I saw it. The Germans realised the importance of Sheffield then, just as they did in the Second World War, when the city was bombed again and many lives were unfortunately lost.

Back at our next point, the police box at the bottom of Staniforth Road, the phone was ringing and we were asked if we could assist. Someone had seen a man take off his clothes, put them in a pile on the canal bank and then throw himself into the water – and he had not surfaced. The divisional car had gone to the scene with a grappling hook and a not-so-new policewoman, who felt she ought to have the experience. If the poor man was dead she needed to be shown how to deal with the body. 'Good for her, that's brave,' I thought to myself as I remembered my own first sudden death. It shouldn't be messy. If he'd only just gone into the water he'd still be on the bottom. After a few days a body fills with gas and comes up to the surface and, if not spotted for a week or two, can be very messy to deal with and identify.

In this case, however, there was a neat pile of clothes with a house brick on top and underneath the brick was a suicide note. I've always said that if you've got the guts to commit suicide, then you've got the guts to live. But never having been in that tenuous position myself I don't really know.

I've dealt with quite a few suicides over the years; overdoses, hangings, plastic bag over the head, the slashing of wrists and throats and even a head in a gas oven (when it was coal gas – unlike now). One suicide involved a butcher who took the guard off his bacon slicer, put his head on the steel block and ran the circular slicer into his neck, severing the jugular vein. Another was a poor woman who had cut her wrists and her throat. When we examined the body at the mortuary it was discovered that she had forty-two scabbed-over cuts all the way up her left arm and twenty-seven on her right arm, as well as six or seven on her throat. The poor lass must have been in turmoil for a week or two – Shall I? Shan't I? Will it hurt? – and so on. No one there to help her, it was pitiful to see and it left me feeling sad for ages. All these things teach you the value of life and to try and be more attentive if someone needs to talk to you. Too many times have I heard people say to someone with a problem, 'I know.' But they don't know and just can't be bothered to listen to someone who may need help.

The canal wasn't very deep but you couldn't see the bottom because the water was a browny orange colour and full of toxins from all the barge traffic which plied the waterway with iron, coal and steel. The banks were fairly steep on either side and the man who'd seen him jump in had gone to work, so we didn't know exactly where to begin our search.

The grappling hook was a bit like a small anchor and was attached to a long length of chain by a steel ring. Having a man at either side of the canal, each holding the chain, meant that by pulling backwards or forwards you could dredge the bottom of the canal with the hook itself going from one side of the bank to the other. You then walked to your left or right repeating the process in the hope of finding him with the hook. It was fairly hit-and-miss and if we couldn't get him it would be a day or two before he would surface. With the banks being steep it was a struggle. If we hooked anything each of us had to walk backwards up the bank in order to get the object out of the water and then high enough out to reach the canal path and on to the bank side. It was far too strenuous a job for the policewoman who was standing near the top of the bank and, if we did find the body, the weight would probably pull her in anyway.

We knew who he was, where he lived and that his parents were both gone. He'd given us all this information in his suicide note and, therefore, it was relatively simple for her first job of that kind.

Pulling the chain was heavy going but after a few minutes we were in luck, or so we thought. Each of us walked backwards up the slope, the water surface broke and there on the hook was an old push-bike, just like my old one but painted black, not pink and yellow. We unhooked it and started again. This time it was heavier, a big old Silver Cross pram with some bricks in it (I suppose to make it sink). This was followed by an old zinc bath and we were getting knackered.

After a rest we started again, and again we felt something on the hook. This time it was something really heavy and we struggled to climb the bank backwards. Fourth time lucky, the body came out of the water, face down, and folded like a jackknife. 'Bloody hell, we've hooked him up his arse.' As the divisional car driver said this, I heard a little moan and a whooshing noise. The policewoman had fainted at the sight and rolled past me and into the canal. She somehow went in feet first. I dropped the chain and the body went back into the canal. What a carry-on! PC Pretentious was already on the canal path and she nearly took him in as well. He managed to grab the collar of her tunic and held on until we both lifted her out. She was lucky she was only wet from the shoulders down and hadn't swallowed any water. She was okay, just embarrassed, which she had no reason to be. The policewoman was good at her job and dead bodies are bad enough anyway, never mind seeing your first one rise out of the water like a fish on a hook.

Because of the polluted water the policewoman was taken to the Northern General Hospital for an injection as a safety precaution, whilst PC Pretentious and I got the body out of the water. It was, luckily for us, still on the hook. A local doctor pronounced him dead and the body was removed to the mortuary. Full credit to the policewoman, who went home, got changed and then went back to the mortuary to deal with the incident. Everybody was chuffed for her, she had proved herself in difficult circumstances and not one person ribbed her. She was one of the team.

Back at the nick and before signing off I had a chat with PC Pretentious. 'Why did they send you to Attercliffe Division?'

'They said it would make me or break me,' he replied.

'Is it like what you thought it would be?'

'Completely different to what I expected. I can't believe what's happened today and I've had a laugh and enjoyed it.'

'Welcome to The Cliffe, mate. You're not at school now – its "mester" time, not playtime.' He laughed at that point and I knew that he would be okay and survive. We worked together on several occasions during his first two years and you could see him maturing by the day. He was a very intelligent chap but now he didn't tell you so. I've never been a gaffer's man and when he rose through the ranks to become a Chief Inspector he rang me and, even though I had then left the job, took me out for a pint, shook my hand and said, 'You taught me that it was important to become a bobby before becoming a sergeant. You were right, thank you.'

He became a good gaffer and everyone respected him. His

parting words to me that night were, 'Do you remember what you said to me at the end of my first shift?'

'Mostly, but maybe not all,' I said, and I related what I could remember; then he told me that the last line was: 'I'm not buttering you up [remembering the café], you'll go down like a bomb [the hand grenade]; and not any body [in the canal] could have done that on their first day.'

CHAPTER THIRTEEN

Cop for That

On 31 May 1967, Sheffield City Police Force ceased to exist. On the next day it amalgamated with the old Rotherham Borough Police Force, becoming known as the Sheffield and Rotherham Constabulary. This force operated until 31 March 1974, after which South Yorkshire Police was born.

In 1962 or '63, I'm not sure which year exactly, the then Chief Constable of Sheffield City Police Force, Eric Staines, got all the police force who weren't on duty together for a meeting in a large hall somewhere in the city. One of the things he said stuck in my mind, even though at the time it didn't mean much to me. This is what he said: 'Ladies and gentlemen, very shortly the country's police forces will be run by politicians and not by chief constables, with the assistance of the police watch committees. People who have never even been to Sheffield, never mind understand its needs, will dictate to us what we do. At that point, ladies and gentlemen, we might as well all go home!' What did he mean? It was many years later, when I could look back at the changes that had taken place and compare things, that I understood more of what he meant.

Not long after the Chief Constable's announcement I was working the night shift in Attercliffe. It was very quiet; it was the works annual shutdown which lasted for two weeks. Many thousands of people had gone on holiday to places as far afield as Cleethorpes, Mablethorpe, Skegness and Blackpool; and the caravan sites would be bursting at the seams. The people who could afford to go on holiday had been saving up all year round and the kids were very excited. For those who hadn't saved up, there was always the feast or fairground on the wasteland near the dog track at the end of Poole Road, Darnall. The many parks around Sheffield would be busy and buses and trains to Derbyshire would be packed with day trippers. This was also a very busy time for the outside contractors. It would give them a chance to make a financial killing. There were only two weeks in which to reline the furnaces and complete necessary repairs, along with the industrial painting. Experience had also taught us as a police division that this was a time when a lot of the works were at their most vulnerable. People often returned to work after the holiday to find that things had been stolen.

We had recently been equipped with Morris Minor Panda cars instead of the motorbikes but this only applied to certain outlying beats. Some of our lads were also on holiday, so I was covering more than one beat and had the use of the Panda car. I headed at first for Tinsley, up and down the side streets containing large and small works. The area was very quiet apart from the odd car or two and an occasional works cat crossing the road. I made my way to the newly erected Tinsley viaduct which had just opened. Watching it slowly being built had been fascinating and now, at last, it was open and the M1 Motorway was complete, running from London through to Leeds.

It was about midnight as I drove along the bottom deck towards Meadow Bank and there wasn't another car to be seen. When I got to the middle of the bridge I stopped the vehicle and got out to take a view of what was below, at the same time noticing several cars on the opposite carriageway driving in the other direction. As I stepped onto the pavement of the bridge I nearly passed out. The bridge was bouncing up and down. I was back in the car like a flash and raced to the Meadow Bank end of the bridge with the police radio in my hand, ready to tell Control that the bridge was about to collapse. Still holding the radio, I stopped myself from using it for a minute. There were cars still on the road and it had only been open a couple of days, so how could it collapse? The other carriageway was exactly the same when I got out on that one and then I remembered something I'd read in the *Star* newspaper. It was a box girder bridge and supported at either end on massive roller bearings. Without these rollers allowing movement, the bridge would collapse.

There was a 50 mph speed limit on the bottom deck of the bridge when it opened, with signs along its length. One day I drove along it at 60 mph in the police car and, idly, everyone overtook me. But if I drove across it at exactly 30 mph, no one overtook me. How strange.

It was by now about 1 am and I made my way back down towards The Cliffe, looking for anything unusual. The divisional boundary was at Washford Bridge, to the right of which were numerous works both large and small. I slowly drove down Stevenson Road and into Birch Road. Both were very narrow and there was the odd gas lamp shining on the cobbled street. Turning left, I saw a large lorry, laden with metal, pull out of a large steelworks and thought nothing of it. It was always a hive of activity at these works but as I drove past the big main gates I saw a man about to close them. He was short and stout and wearing a 'nick hat' (trilby) and as he closed the gate I got a glimpse of his face under the gas lamp. He was one of the biggest suspected metal thieves in the city. At the same time I realised that there were no workers' cars parked on the street, so the firm must be shut down. I wondered what he was up to. I was about to pull up and investigate when I thought of the lorry that had just left the premises. Should I grab the little guy? The lorry might be legitimate and nothing to do with 'Shorty' and by the time I'd checked it out Shorty would have gone. My instinct told me to go for the lorry.

I raced down East Coast Road to the main Brightside Lane. Left, right or straight on? He was nowhere to be seen. For both left and right I could see a fair way, but he wasn't there; straight on I could only see a fairly short distance to the top of a hill. I had to gamble and drove straight on. The car engine was screaming as I flew over the hill to a crossroads. Again three choices: left, right or straight on. As I was just past the Corner Pin pub I noticed a dimly lit cobbled street to my left and thought I saw a brake light come on in the distance. The tyres shrieked as I turned the car round. I was out of our area now and didn't know where I really was. I saw a sign saying Forncet Street and raced along there, with the blackness of the works all around me. There were big and medium-sized lorries parked along the road, left, I suppose, for the two-week holiday period as there were no lights or people anywhere.

Slamming the brakes on, I put the car into reverse and sped backwards. Had I passed it or was I seeing things? I jumped out of the car and there it was, still with its engine running and the driver's door half open, which it hadn't been a few seconds before. I'd been right to follow the lorry after all, even though the bird had flown. I shone my torch up and down but to no avail. He could be anywhere, it was so dark. There was no radio reception, so I'd have to lock the lorry up and call for assistance from somewhere else.

I was about to grab the cab door when it hit me hard and full in the face, knocking me onto the cobbled street. The man looked as big as a gorilla as he leapt out of the lorry and started legging it towards the city. The blood was pouring from my nose and mouth where the door had hit me and later I found out that I had two teeth missing. I felt dazed as I got up and slowly set off after him. As he passed under the light of a gas lamp I could see from his build that he'd never be an Olympic runner, but he also looked a toughy. I let him have his run in the hope that he'd have no energy left with which to fight. Another 100 yards and he was slowing and within seconds he was moving at a crawl.

Our instructions when using a truncheon were to hit the elbow, collar bone, ankle or knee in order to disable the culprit. Even though he had smashed my face with the lorry door (bigger than a truncheon), I wanted to face him man to man. He was bigger than me. He knew his freedom was at stake so he was obviously not going to give in easily, but the truncheon remained in my trouser pocket.

He was bending down now with his hands on his knees and trying to get his breath back. I didn't have the chance to tell him he was under arrest, he came straight at me, head-butted me in the stomach and at the same time I took one on my right temple. He was a fighter all right, but it takes two to tango.

'If that's the way you want it, mate, I'm your man!' I must have looked like a loser – a busted nose, split lips, two teeth missing, a shiner coming up on my right eye and covered in blood and, to make matters worse, I hadn't struck a blow. I was mad now and it was my turn. I'd taken two or three paces back and waited for him. He came charging at me like a bull and roaring like a lion and with his head slightly lowered. Whack, what a pearler. It sent shock waves through my hand and arm and I thought I'd broken both. He went down like a ton of bricks and didn't even twitch. He was out cold.

I didn't even know where I was in this industrial bit of the city but I could see a pub on the corner of a street, about twenty-five yards away. I dragged my guy across to it by his coat collar and rang a bell on the door jamb. It seemed to take for ever for the lights to come on and then a chap in pyjamas looked through the window. Seeing my uniform he opened the door and looked at us both and then rang for help at my request. Within five or ten minutes both uniform and CID lads arrived from West Bar and, at the same time, laddo was coming round and looked as if he was about to have another go. One of the lads drew his truncheon. 'Use that on him, mate, and I'll use it on you,' I said sharply. 'He's my prisoner, handcuff him and he'll be okay, but don't you dare manhandle him.'

'Sorry, pal, but he's knocked a lot of our lads about in his time,' said the PC. 'I know who he is and I know his form and he's coming with me, okay?'

The CID lads took him back to Attercliffe and, after thanking the landlord, I walked back to the police car. The lorry engine was still running and the dented door was wide open. I managed a wry smile to myself. What if Shorty had run after us, seen what was happening and then driven off in the lorry; now that would have been embarrassing, with no evidence.

Back at the nick I told my story to the CID lads including the bit about Shorty at the gates, who was a well-known associate of the prisoner. Both specialised in the theft of high-value metals. Both men were single and a visit to Shorty's house showed that there was no one there. The curtains were open even though it was about 4 am, which was odd – or was it? He was circulated on the wanted list, so all we could do was wait until he was found and arrested. We didn't have to wait long. At about 6.30 am there was a call from the police in Mablethorpe. They asked if we were looking for a man called —— ——? 'Yes, why?' I said.

'He's smashed a few shop windows in Mablethorpe and given himself up, said he was drunk. We've charged him with malicious damage.'

I told him the story and asked him to find out what he was doing in Mablethorpe. A little while later came the reply. 'He says he had been staying with his sister's family in a caravan. I've been to see the sister and both her and her husband backed up his story.'

The crafty little so-and-so must have raced home after seeing me and, realising what could happen, opened his curtains before driving to Mablethorpe. He must have seen his sister first and then smashed the windows later, giving himself up to the police just to get an alibi. He was a professional for sure, but there was still a twist in the tale.

Under interview by CID the big man said nothing and denied even knowing Shorty and, at that time, he didn't know that his mate had not been locked up. The CID lads were good and at some stage in the inquiry the big lad was asked why he thought we were onto them so quickly. It couldn't be coincidence, the odds were too great, someone must have tipped us off, but who? Shorty hadn't been seen since. The cogs apparently started to turn and then: 'That little bastard grassed me up! I should have known better, we've been planning that job for weeks.'

Brilliant, what a cough (admission). The big fella grassed Shorty up for some jobs he'd done on his own and a lot of stolen metal was later recovered. It also transpired that there was a second lorry in the works yard waiting to be driven away by Shorty after the big fella left, but he panicked when he saw me and tried to pretend he was the gateman.

The company was pleased we'd foiled the job, which was good for all of us. The two men were charged with breaking and entering and the big lad with theft of a lorry, driving whilst disqualified, no insurance ... and assaulting me. The contents of the lorry were valued at about £40,000 – a huge sum of money in those days. They both had previous convictions and the big lad got four years' imprisonment and Shorty got three years. What did I get? A dental bill and the satisfaction of seeing the kink in the big man's nose a few years later when he came out. I never saw Shorty again but I can't for the life of me think why. Oh, and I also got a commendation from the Chief Constable which read: 'For keen observation and prompt action'.

Progress had brought us the Panda car and I must admit that we wouldn't have nailed Little and Large without it. As I drove around in one, though, I couldn't help feeling for the people we were paid to help. The little old lady who wanted to talk or the children with sweets for the policeman they used to say hello to in the street, but who now drove past them. I wondered if that's what the politicians were wanting, the loss of the personal touch. Maybe that's what Eric Staines, the old Chief Constable, meant. I didn't know any politicians so I'd have to wait until I met one and then decide for myself if they wanted me to be a proper bobby or just a cardboard cut-out.

The definition of a policeman's job then was the protection of life and property and the prevention of and detection of crime. In my opinion one of the best ways to detect crime was by talking and listening to people on your patch. If you were right with them then they would be right with you. Driving a car meant that you didn't speak to as many people as you did on the beat and so didn't learn as much either.

I remember one time, whilst walking the beat, I was told about a lad who was using a car that had run out of road tax. The lad was a bit of a tearaway and an ex-biker, so I checked it out. The tax had indeed run out but everything else was in order and so I employed another tactic to see what would happen. I said to the lad, 'Look, you've no tax and I've got a problem.'

'What is it?' he asked.

'This last few weeks there have been several thefts of motorbikes on my patch, which doesn't make me happy.'

'Why are you telling me this?' he asked, bemused.

'You tax your car and I'll forget about it if you find the man who's nicking them. You've got one week.' He nodded. I knew that he would have to tax the car now anyway and I might get a bonus. I didn't have to wait a week. He came to Darnall section station and found me.

'I've taxed the car. Thanks.' And as he went he passed me an envelope which contained two names and three addresses. I knew the two names and addresses but the third was a lock-up garage near the dog track. Later that evening, and in my off-duty time, I sat in my own car and I waited for the lads to come to the garage, which they did. I recovered six stolen motorbikes and the lads got nine months in prison each. And it all started with someone telling the bobby on the beat a story. Had I been in a car we would never have spoken and the crime might never have been solved.

CHAPTER FOURTEEN

A Funny Old Day

Being a policeman meant that you never knew what you were going to have to deal with next. The radio message always seemed to start in the same way: 'Go to ... and deal with ...' You always held your breath as to what was ahead. It could be absolutely anything: a pub fight, a stolen car, someone seen breaking in, a shoplifter at such-and-such, a report of a person missing – and so on. Because of the nature of the job we were never asked to attend to anything 'nice' and as we were a large division within the city we were constantly on the go, especially if you were assigned to a motorcycle or a car beat. The calls we dreaded most were road traffic accidents (RTAs) and sudden deaths. An RTA could vary from a simple knock to a serious or fatal injury, whilst a sudden death could vary from a recent and clean one to someone who had been dead for a while, which could be very unpleasant.

I'd just picked up the Panda car at Attercliffe police station and was making my way to the busy beats of the Manor, where the afternoon shift (3 pm to 11 pm) was always hectic. I was showing PC Pretentious the area and its parameters. He'd mellowed a bit by now and was easier to get on with. Just then the radio went. We had only been on duty ten minutes.

'Go to Nidd Road and deal with a road traffic accident.'

'Here we go, mate.'

Nidd Road is a long cobbled street but quiet, especially on a sunny Saturday afternoon.

'Let's hope it's not a child who's got knocked down.'

PC Pretentious agreed. A couple of minutes later we turned into Nidd Road with our blue light flashing but there was no one to be seen anywhere. I switched off the light and drove up and down the street slowly. There was no sign of a damaged vehicle anywhere. It was odd. The street itself consisted of a long row of terraced houses on either side of the road, so we checked the numbers, looking for the address that Control had given us. The front door of the relevant house was wide open and, a few seconds later, I was knocking on it. A male voice from within shouted, 'Hello.'

'Have you reported an accident?' I asked.

'Aye, come on in.'

It was a typical terraced house and, as we walked in, you could see that the usual sideboard was on the back wall to my left and a settee to my right. The middle door leading to the kitchen was open, as was the back door, which meant that, from the front door, you could see through the house and into the back yard.

'Come on in and sit down, lads. Mary, put kettle on, love.'

The old chap was in his chair watching his black and white television and across from him was a young chap sat on a stool.

'Sit on t'settee, lads, you'll have a brew in a minute.'

'A brew would be great but why are we here?' I asked.

Mary had arrived with the tea, a mug each for the old man and his mate, but we were each treated to a Royal Albert cup and saucer, which, as it turned out, was part of a tea set the old chap had received as a retirement gift when he left Bone Cravens up the road.

'He's a right drama queen,' said Mary. 'Tell 'em what happened.'

'Well, me and our Mary were sat on t'settee watching a cowboy film, when we heard a funny noise behind us. We looked at each other and I said, "I'm sure that were a motorbike that's come through t'sitting room and into t'kitchen," and when we looked it was, but he'd gone through t'kitchen as well and into t'back yard. It were a good job it's hot and we'd got all our doors open.'

Both PC Pretentious and I were open-mouthed in disbelief and I asked if anyone was hurt. The lad on the stool answered.

'No. I managed to stop before I hit the wall in the backyard.'

'How did it happen?'

'I was riding down the road nice and steady like, when a dog flew out of the entry. I swerved to miss it and, luckily for me, all three doors were open and I ended up riding straight through front room, into t'back room and out of t'back door and into t'yard. I'm ever so sorry, officer.'

We couldn't believe what we were hearing; I checked the bike and there was not a scratch on it. He'd driven through the front door and through the gap between the front of the sideboard and the back of the settee, through the kitchen and into the yard. The only damage was to one of the drop handles on one of the sideboard drawers, which had broken off when he caught it with his brake lever.

'It was my fault anyway,' said the old man, whose name was Albert. 'It was my dog, he doesn't like the sound of motorbikes.'

It's not very often that you can have a laugh when dealing with a road traffic accident but this was certainly one of the quirkiest ones that I ever had to deal with and every time I thought about it afterwards I'd burst into fits of laughter.

The radio again: 'Attend Hastilar Road. A neighbour

reporting that her next-door neighbour hasn't been seen for two days, will you investigate?'

This was not a blue light job; it sounded as if we were too late for that. The lady who'd phoned in was outside the house along with a group of other neighbours and, when we arrived, they pointed out the house concerned. I could see that the curtains were closed, even though it was 4.30 in the afternoon.

'Something's been troubling him lately and I think he's done something to himself,' said the old lady. Knocking loudly on both front and back doors produced nothing and no one had a key or was aware of any relatives of the man, so there was only one thing for it. Past experience told me that some doors would give easier than others, but until you tried them you never knew which ones. If the man was dead inside so be it, but if he was in a collapsed state he needed help urgently.

I ran hard at the back door with my shoulder and, with a mighty crash, it went first time and we were in. 'That noise would have woken even the dead,' I said to PC Pretentious, who gave a tight smile. I could tell that, like me, he wasn't looking forward to our task. We shouted again but to no avail and at the same time opened the curtains to let in the light, but there was no one in the kitchen. We walked gingerly into the sitting room, but that was also empty, as was a bottle of whisky on the table, but no glass. After all the noise we'd made, why were we tiptoeing upstairs and trying to be quiet? I'll never know, but we did.

The bathroom was empty. I opened the door of the big bedroom, and there he was. He must have died in his sleep. I could only just see the top of his head as he lay under the bed covers. We were discussing what to do next as I pulled back the bed covers in order to check for any signs of life, while PC Pretentious opened the curtains.

Without warning the poor man sat bolt upright in bed whilst two uniformed policemen plastered themselves to the ceiling of his bedroom, having leapt there in fright. He wasn't dead and he wasn't happy.

He grabbed two large hearing aids off the bedside cabinet and put them in his ears. 'What the bleeding hell are you two doing in my house, never mind my bedroom?'

'We had a report that you had not been seen and might be ill and want assistance,' I replied.

'I've not been well but that's no business of yours anyway.'

'We thought you might want some help, so we knocked and shouted but you didn't answer.'

'I'm stone bloody deaf, that's why, and I've had two or three whiskies to make me sleep better. Is that a crime?' He was really mad.

The old chap was out of bed now and stood there in his pyjamas while he fished his false teeth out of a glass at the side of his bed and put them in his mouth. Then I suddenly remembered that his back door was smashed and hanging off its hinges.

'Who sent for you anyway? I'll bet it's that nosey old cow from next door. She always wants to know your business.'

When we got downstairs and he saw the back door the balloon really went up.

'What the bloody hell's happened here?' he shouted. I started to explain but the gentleman didn't want to know.

'It's a bit of a bugger. I don't feel well and have a whisky or two and go to bed and then when I wake up I think I'm dreaming. All I can see is two hairy-arsed coppers with a look of terror on their faces.' Both PC Pretentious and I said sorry at the same time. 'Then I come downstairs and find half me house has been knocked down – bloody hellfire.' With that he went for his whisky bottle, which of course was empty. Between me and PC Pretentious we had enough money for a quarter bottle of whisky and I sent him to the shop to buy it for the old chap. In the meantime I got the Public Works Department out to replace the door. We were lucky they had an office and joiners 200 yards from where we were. We apologised and left him with his whisky and the joiner, who was also getting an ear-bashing. For the second time that afternoon we were both hysterical, but this time we were both skint as well.

We were just finishing our snap at Elm Tree sub-station when the landline telephone rang.

'Attend road traffic accident Prince of Wales Road, outside Pipworth Road School, ambulance in attendance and it sounds serious.' Grabbing our helmets we were off, blue light flashing. At the scene was an ambulance and they were just putting an injured man inside. I had a quick look and he appeared to be in a bad way. There was blood everywhere and he had suffered serious lacerations to the head and face and I could only see one eye. It was an emergency and there was no time to search his pockets for identification, which would be done later. I spoke to the driver of the only car involved and asked him what had happened. He was obviously badly shaken up but managed to tell me that a few minutes before the accident he was taking his wife to work at Manor Top when he saw a man staggering about on the pavement. He thought he was drunk. On his way back down Prince of Wales Road he looked for but couldn't see the man, but fifty yards further on, as he was passing a parked car, the man stumbled out in front of it and right in front of him. He hit the man, who flew up the bonnet and through the windscreen of the vehicle. This story was also backed up by two independent witnesses.

After taking details and measurements at the scene we went to the hospital. The man was in intensive care but was expected to make a full recovery. The staff at the hospital had found his details and informed relatives, who were going to have to travel a fair way to see him. The doctor also told us that he was intoxicated. So what with that and the independent witnesses' statements, the accident appeared to be the man's fault, but we would have to interview him later if he survived.

We were at the end of our shift now and PC Pretentious said, 'Is it always like this?'

'You are joking? Two fun ones and one bad one, I don't think you'll get that again in a hurry.' I know I didn't.

The following morning was a nice sunny Sunday and I wasn't working until 3 pm. That is until one of the lads called round to see me. The duty inspector had made an 11 am appointment at the Northern General Hospital for me to meet the wife of the man who had been injured in the accident the night before. This had never happened before and the inspector wouldn't have made the decision lightly. I was intrigued and it probably meant that I could finish at 7 pm and have a beer and a game of crib at the pub after work.

The wife seemed a very nice and ordinary woman and thanked me for coming to see her. I asked about her husband and she replied, 'I want to first tell you a story and then ask you for a favour please.' This is what she told me: 'I married my husband about thirty-five years ago and we lived very happily together. We had two children who are now grown up and have children of their own but they have never seen their grandfather. About twenty-two years ago he had an accident in the steelworks. His face was badly scarred and he lost an eye as well. He felt really depressed and started to get jealous of me because of his disfigurement. He thought I didn't love him any more and he used to fly into a rage if anyone mentioned his eye. He got worse and worse until I had to leave him. In order to survive he took in a lodger who was Russian and every time the Russian got drunk he would torment my husband about his eye. It got to a stage where he couldn't take any more and, one night when the Russian was drunk and tormenting him, he waited until he fell asleep in the chair.' At that point she went quiet and I saw that she was crying.

'What happened then?' I gently asked.

'He lost control and smashed the man's head in with a hammer and then fetched the police. Normally he wouldn't have hurt a fly. He went to prison for fifteen years after admitting murder and he was released yesterday morning. I still love him and always have and we were due to meet today for reconciliation with all the family.'

'How can I help?'

'He's never been a big drinker and, from what I can gather, he went to look at our old house yesterday after drinking five or six pints to celebrate his release. That's a lot for him, he never had more than three before and he's not had one for fifteen years. He tried to cross the road to look at his old school, but before he went to prison there was hardly any traffic and he couldn't cope with it and got himself knocked down.'

'So what is the favour?' I asked.

'He's progressing very well, the doctor says, and he'll be out in about a week, but his glass eye is missing and he's very, very frustrated without it.'

'I'll go to the scene and see what I can find, okay?'

'Thank you again, officer.' And off I went. What a story.

The car driver concerned had instinctively swerved to the right as he hit the man and then stopped on the very wide grass verge which separated the carriageways. I must have searched the area for an hour without any success and began to wonder if it was in the car. I checked my pocket book, where I had written down the driver's details, and realised that he only lived about four miles away. It was out of our division but, after getting the okay from the office, I was off.

I turned into a fairly large cul-de-sac, with well-kept detached houses. There weren't many of them down The Cliffe. I was in a posh area now. The car involved was parked on my right and the driver was sitting on a low wall surrounding his neat garden. I got out of my vehicle and he jumped up to greet me.

'Am I glad to see you! I've just had to send for the midwife, who lives a few roads away,' he said.

'Congratulations, will it be your first baby?'

'No, the wife's not pregnant.'

'Why send for the midwife then?'

'I couldn't think of anyone else.'

I could see that he was agitated.

'Look at that,' he said, pointing through the open car door. There on the floor amongst the broken glass was the eye and I realised then that the poor chap thought it was real. I picked it up and he was sick over his wall. As I said farewell I put the eye on my car's front passenger seat in the bottom half of a matchbox. Every time I turned a corner it moved and looked for all the world as if it was winking at me.

The man's wife was still at the hospital when I got back and she couldn't thank me enough. I gave her the eye (so to speak) and a week later her husband was discharged. Every time I go up Prince of Wales Road I think about them and hope that they are still happy together. The driver of the car was exonerated of all blame and that night I had four pints and won 40 pence at crib.

There were several comments at work from the lads when I bumped into them, such as 'Eye, eye', 'Socket to me', 'Wink, wink', 'I'll keep my eye out for you' and so on.

I checked up the lady's story later. Her hubby really had killed a Russian with a hammer and had just finished a fifteen-year stretch in prison.

CHAPTER FIFTEEN

Busy Shifts, Great Characters and Pelé

As far as I was concerned, the night shift was always more interesting than days and afternoons. I loved working Darnall and Attercliffe best of all because they were foot beats unless someone was off and then you used the car.

It was just a normal weekday night as I walked to Darnall Terminus to survey the comings and goings. 11 pm was pub 'turning-out time', when most of the drinkers would make their way home quietly. There were more people about than usual, including couples who would normally only go out on a Friday or Saturday night. It wasn't Christmas or a Bank Holiday so what was happening? I stood where I could be seen in order to check what sort of mood they were in and everyone was happy, but drunk. It was like Christmas Eve and as a couple walked towards me the lady said, 'Evening, occifer, I'll bet you've got a big truncheon,' and then fits of laughter as if she thought that it was the first time I'd heard it. 'You've got a bobby's job, mate.'

'Yes, but it's not much cop though,' I replied – and you knew what was coming next, much to the poor old husband's embarrassment.

'I've always wanted to kiss a bobby.' If she had been nineteen or similar it wouldn't have been so bad but it was always the ones about sixty to seventy years old.

'What's going off tonight, pal?' I asked the poor husband, who was doing his best to get his wife home.

'Everybody's had a win on Harry Hodge's horse. It's won at 50 to 1.'

It turned out that one of the big scrap dealers had told a couple of his mates in Frank's barber's shop that his horse was 'trying' that day. The two mates had told two more, who also told two more and so on, and it seemed like all Darnall had put a bet on it. Fancy, winning at 50 to 1, I'd have had a nicker on that myself if I'd known. There was no trouble and eventually everyone dispersed. All you could hear around Darnall was heavy snoring.

I checked the shops on the terminus and down Staniforth Road for any signs of burglary but all was clear. On the way back up the other side of the road it was a different story. The rear window of the newsagent's had been smashed and there was blood all over the sill on the outside, but none on the inside, so whoever it was had not been able to get in and was injured as well. I followed the trail of blood, which was substantial, along Main Road for about 100 yards, until I saw a man lying face down on the pavement. There was a large gash along his neck and blood everywhere. He was unconscious and in a bad way. I ran to a phone box and rang for an ambulance and, under the light of my torch, I could see that it was a well-known local criminal, who had only come out of prison three weeks before for shop-breaking. The ambulance took him to hospital and when he was released a few days later he was arrested by the CID lads. He'd smashed the bottom half of the sash window, undone the top half by releasing the catch and slid the bottom half up in order to gain access. Unfortunately for him he pushed his head through the window and the broken glass fell out and onto his neck, creating a guillotine effect. The man was very lucky that night. If we had been covering the beat with a car I doubt if he would have been found and he could easily have died.

It was now 2.10 am and snap-time was 3 am. I made my way to Ike Worrall's bread shop, near the Co-op at the bottom of Main Road and Waverley Road. The bakehouse was at the back of the shop and Ike did all the baking himself. His work would start at 10 pm, six nights a week and he worked fourteen hours a day. Ike was a small, wiry man and very fit. There was more fat on a cold chip than there was on him. I mashed the two of us a mug of tea and then took off my helmet and tunic, replacing the latter with a white smock.

The alarm on the very large oven sounded and I opened the door. The smell of freshly baked bread was wonderful. Several dozen loaves were all lined up in their separate tins and, using the special long-handled, flat-bladed paddle, I carefully removed them all and put them on a big table to cool. As the last one came out Ike replaced it with another batch and shut the oven. As I knocked the edge of the tins on the table to release the bread ready for stacking in the shop, Ike was mixing the dough in a large cauldron-like machine. He would then put the dough into a big round dish and pull down the lid, which segmented the dough into twenty-four separate small pieces. Each of these he rolled in flour and within seconds they became unbaked breadcakes. He was a brilliant bloke and a one-man production line; what a worker. Many's the time when I finished work I would deliver his bread for him round Darnall, Handsworth and the Manor, just to give him a break, and my reward was a freshly baked loaf for Mrs Proctor.

This morning I'd been there for about fifteen minutes when Ike took some bread into the front shop, which had a glass door. He came straight back into the bakehouse.

'That new sergeant that all you lads hate is hiding in the doorway. He must have seen you come in.'

'Thanks, Ike,' I said and crept round the shop counter to look. He was right, it was Sergeant Double-Dyed Bastard. He was really sneaky and would stab anyone in the back to get on, which he did. He became a chief inspector somewhere, at a young age. I was due back at Darnall sub-station in five minutes and he had me trapped.

Back in the bakehouse I grabbed my helmet and tunic and, with the use of Ike's stepladder, climbed up the wall and shinned along it to an outhouse. I went up and over the roof and onto another wall. This was the back wall of the Co-op and it was covered in barbed wire so I had to get off, quickly. There was an old display unit in the yard, which I dragged to the gate and within seconds I climbed up it and over the top of the gate, which brought me into Waverley Road. The sub-station was in darkness as it should be and, when I opened the door, the clock said 3.01 am. I grabbed a plate, sprinkled breadcrumbs on it and the skin of my banana and waited, pretending to be asleep. Sure enough, ten minutes later in walked Sergeant Sneaky and coughed to wake me up. I pretended to jump and his mouth kept opening and then closing without speaking. His little plan had failed and he knew it. Even the gaffers disliked him. At 10.55 pm he would lock up anyone for anything just to get four hours' paid overtime. He didn't last long down The Cliffe though, we all made sure of that, and it was more relaxed again when Sergeant Johnny No Mates had gone.

*

One of the lads had taken four hours' leave so I took over the car for the rest of the shift and worked three beats. I went down Darnall Road to the brickworks on Makin Road to hopefully see an old pal whom I hadn't seen for a while. I climbed up the wooden steps to the top level and said hello to the nightwatchman, old Tom. I always found it fascinating when I visited him. Tom had a little cabin and in it was a chair, table, radio and kettle. Stretching away in front of this cabin for quite a distance was a red-brick floor covered in brick dust and set into the floor at regular intervals were round iron lids about six inches across, with a hook on them. There were dozens and underneath were the brick kilns. Every time the temperature of the kilns dropped to a certain level it was Tom's job to lift the lids and drop a small quantity of coal down each hole, which glowed red hot when opened. I could never stand it for too long, it was too hot for me. After a chat I asked if Fred was downstairs and he answered in the affirmative.

Back downstairs I walked through one of the open archways and towards the kilns. It was lovely and warm and also quiet. My feet didn't make a sound as I walked through the warm sand on the floor. Fred was fast asleep when I found him, stood with his arms looped over a clothes line that he'd rigged up between two hooks. I'd seen this before in a registered doss house in Barnsley when I was younger – where a sign said '1/- per night for a bed' but if you 'dossed' on a clothes line it was free. This is where the expression 'I could sleep on a clothes line' comes from. Fred was a proper old-fashioned tramp who lived out on the road and I had first met him about three years before when two youths were tormenting him. He was a lovely old chap and he wandered all over the place living off the land and doing odd jobs. Every six months or so he'd come to Sheffield and call at the nick and ask for me. I'd always get the same message, 'Fred's in town – says you'll know where he is.' I knew, Tom knew and Fred knew that he shouldn't be in the kilns but Tom and I turned a blind eye to it, especially in winter when he sometimes stayed for a week or two, always sleeping on his clothes line, which he assured me was more comfortable than the floor. We talked about the country, snaring rabbits to eat and using horse-hair stoppers to bag pheasants.

Knowing that he was likely to be there, I had brought him a large pork pie and a bottle of beer, the latter of which he downed with gusto. The only downside for me was that he insisted on making me a brew in his old enamel billycan, which was absolutely loppy. He was, of course, being kind and offering to me the only thing that he had to give in return for the pie and beer. He wiped the rim of the can with a bit of rag produced, I think, from his pocket and gave me the can, saying, 'It's okay, I washed it in a stream last week, it'll not poison thi.' I'd rather have kissed a toad than put my lips on the can but to Fred's delight I managed somehow to get it down and off I went.

The Sheffield wholesale market on the Parkway was busy; it was 5 am and opening time. Streams of vans and pick-ups owned by shopkeepers were trying to be first in the queue at the various outlets, eager to get their produce back to the shops for opening time. The first person I saw was Tony Alexander, a self-employed fish wholesaler. Every other night Tony drove down from Aberdeen in his lorry and dropped off pre-ordered boxes of fish outside the various fish dealers' premises. Tony was a right character. He was as hard as nails, cheerful and witty and always good for a nice piece of fish. His lorry was a real beauty and sometimes when I called in at the market early, I'd drive it round the fish dock and drop off the boxes while he had a thirty-minute kip in my Panda car before his long drive back to Aberdeen. I only saw him every three weeks when I was on night shift. That morning I was driving the lorry round the dock and Tony was in the Panda car. A few minutes later I saw the reflection of a blue flashing light in one of the shop windows and round the corner came my police car, driven by Tony. What the hell's going off, I thought, as he pulled up, grabbed a cardboard box of fish from his lorry and jumped back into the Panda car.

'Martyn, I forgot this special order for a customer in Killamarsh, I'll be back in a bit.' Before I could do or say anything he drove off, lights flashing. What the . . . ? I didn't panic as I thought he'd driven round the corner for a laugh, but he was nowhere to be seen. I drove the lorry to the security office at the front of the market where I could see the watchman, Ken, having a fag and when I jumped out of the cab Ken looked at me in amazement.

'I thought that was you who just left the market with the blue light on. What's going on?'

I was speechless at first, but eventually told Ken the story and we were both stood there in disbelief.

'What if he crashes it?' said Ken.

'I daren't even think about it,' I replied.

'It must be nine or ten miles away from here.'

'I know that! What if the radio goes for me and I can't answer? Put the kettle on, Ken. I can't think straight.'

Ten minutes, fifteen minutes, twenty minutes – nothing, no sign of him. After thirty minutes I was going frantic, thinking he'd get locked up, I'd get locked up and I'd lose my job too. Five minutes later we could see a blue light flashing in the distance and a minute later Tony screeched to a stop outside the security office. He was laughing his head off and totally unconcerned.

'Sorry. I'm a few minutes later than I thought I'd be.'

'You barmy bugger, you'll get me hung! Did anyone see you?' I yelled.

'I only saw one other car there and back – a police patrol car going in the opposite direction to me.'

'You must be joking, what happened?'

'I suppose he thought I was on my way to a job with the

blue light going, he just waved and flashed his lights. Nobody would be daft enough to steal a police car, now would they?'

I was about to go mad at him when he said, 'I'm running a bit late now, I'll see you in a couple of days,' and with that he jumped into his lorry and was off.

'What a nutter,' I thought to myself but I had to smile – with relief.

I called into the bakery on the way home and Ike told me that Sergeant Unpopular had gone into the bakehouse earlier on, looking for one of his officers.

'There's no policemen here, Sergeant, you can see that for yourself.' He had a quick look round and then went away, muttering to himself.

'Thanks, Ike. I can't take your bread this morning, we are all at a big football match this afternoon, at Hillsborough, so I've only got five hours' kip.'

I had never been into football because I had always preferred cricket, unlike all the other bobbies down The Cliffe. Normally there were no problems getting volunteers to police a match at Sheffield Wednesday football ground but if it was a big one we were made to go. This meant that you finished the night shift at 7 am and went to the ground for 1 pm and then back on night shift at 11 pm. The perk, of course, for most of the lads, was being able to watch the match for free. We got our bus fares reimbursed, plus a sandwich, an apple and one whole pound note in cash. Wow. It was a Tuesday and Sheffield

Wednesday were playing a famous team called Santos, from Brazil. At the time a miners' strike and energy crisis (during what was known as 'the winter of discontent') was causing regulated blackouts across the country and, for this reason, the match was brought forward to a 2.30 pm kick-off, thereby avoiding the use of power for floodlights. This also meant that thousands of kids were given time off school in order to watch what I was told would be an important match.

As we were patrolling outside the ground and making sure that there was no trouble with the tens of thousands trying to get through the turnstiles I heard someone shout, 'Uncle Martyn, Uncle Martyn!' After a while I spotted my young nephew Bramwell Towse in the queue. He was about eleven or twelve and looked really excited. I went to talk to him.

'Uncle Martyn, can you get me Pelé's autograph please?'

'Who on earth is Pelé?' I asked. Incredible, I know, but at the time I had never heard of the star of Santos and Brazil. Bramwell's eyes were wide open in amazement.

'He's the best footballer in the world, Uncle Martyn.'

As he went through the turnstile I said that I would do my best and a little later spotted a chap selling souvenirs off a stall. I told him the story and he laughed out loud when I asked if he had a picture of Pelé so that I could identify him.

'You must be the only man in the world who doesn't know what Pelé looks like.' I felt a bit of a twerp, so hurriedly bought a large poster of him and shoved it inside my tunic.

Most people in the massive crowd, about 45,000, were high as kites with excitement as the game kicked off and our instructions, as we sat on little stools around the pitch, were always the same: 'If anyone scores a goal stand up, turn round, face the crowd and glare at them.' When Santos scored the first goal the place erupted and not one of the crowd saw us glaring at them. Another wasted idea by a 'jobsworth', I thought. The atmosphere was fantastic, even though Wednesday lost 2–0. At that point I thought about young Bramwell's request and followed the players down the tunnel and towards the dressing rooms. I knew that there wouldn't be any bother outside as the crowd consisted of only Wednesday supporters. Outside the away players' dressing-room door stood giants – they were in suits and were obviously bodyguards. I wasn't sure what to do, so I took the bull by the horns and walked to the door, only to be stopped by them. Telling them why I was there made no difference at all – they didn't speak English, never mind Barnsley English. Just then a small chap, also in a suit, came to my rescue.

'What do you want?' he said.

I showed him the picture of Pelé and then counted to eleven with my fingers, then I got out my pen and pretended to write my signature on the poster. It worked and you could see from his face that he understood. He simply said, 'Wait,' and lifted his thumb in acknowledgement.

As each player came out the little chap spoke to them and

they signed the poster. I got to ten but no Pelé, so I said to a player, 'Pelé?' and he beckoned me to follow. We went to the dressing-room door where the giants blocked our way. The player was not happy at this and a shouting match, in a foreign language, started, as I just stood there holding the poster. Someone from inside the dressing room shouted and the gorillas opened the door for me and indicated for me to enter, which I did. Pelé greeted me with just a white towel wrapped around his bottom half. Don't ask me how or why because I can't give a definitive answer, but I immediately knew that I was in the presence of a very special person.

'Did you enjoy the game? What family do you have? Is it good being an English policeman?' he asked. He also asked many more questions and seemed genuinely interested in me, a mere PC. I sat and we talked for maybe fifteen minutes and he signed the poster. He was very gracious and he made me feel as if I was the important one rather than the other way round. I was and still am in awe of the man – what an ambassador not only for his sport, but also the human race. Very rarely do we get the chance to meet someone special in our lives but, thanks to Bramwell, I certainly did that day.

Bramwell was over the moon with the poster and as he got older he kindly passed it on to my lads Richard and Paul who have the poster now, even though I creased it by putting it in my tunic. Do you know, they wouldn't part with it for a gold pig.

CHAPTER SIXTEEN

Christmas Cheer – for Some!

During the build-up to Christmas some of us took on different roles, which could be quite diverse. The large parade room at Attercliffe police station had a stage and also a piano. Most of the policemen and policewomen would get together at weekends to rehearse the Attercliffe Christmas pantomime for all the kids. It was great fun and everyone, including the gaffers, mucked in to make it a good do. When it came to being selected for different parts, I thought that I would be the choice for Prince Charming, but no, I had to be satisfied with playing an Ugly Sister or Widow Twanky. My acting career took a big dive when they wouldn't even let me be the front end of the cow in *Jack and the Beanstalk*; instead they made me be the arse end. All the local kids and parents were invited and the atmosphere was fabulous. It was a great public-relations exercise.

Sometimes we were drafted into the city centre for crowd control whilst also keeping an eye out for organised shoplifters and pickpockets who were rife at this time of year. I had never before and never have since seen crowds like them. The main shopping areas in Sheffield, including the markets and the High Street, must have held 100,000 people at any one time on a Saturday. There was no Meadowhall or supermarkets and Christmas shopping didn't start in September like it does now. It was more like the second week in December when the goodies came into the shops and the workers got paid. The Salvation Army band would play Christmas carols and the atmosphere was superb. It brought back memories of when I was young.

At the age of about thirteen I used to walk to the pit to meet my dad, Fred. All the miners at Houghton Main finished work at lunchtime on Christmas Eve. The three-mile walk to the pit seemed to take minutes because I was so excited. It was 'Bull' week. This meant that as well as a normal week's pay the men also got paid for all the overtime they'd worked in the last month or two.

I waited for Dad at the bottom of the railway bridge steps, next to the pit baths, longing for him to come over the bridge. The miners were half a mile underground and they were brought up from the bowels of the earth in a cage, in batches. He was lucky, he was in the first cage, along with about another forty men. Dad, like the others, was as black as the ace of spades from the coal dust clinging to the sweat on his body. The men's pit lamps were still lit and to a man they ran over the bridge laughing and singing, towards the red-brick wall of the bath house. I knew what was going to happen next, I'd seen it before. Each one of them reached upwards and recovered two matches and one cigarette, which they had hidden in gaps in the wall — their first cigarette for eight hours. After a fag and a bath Dad queued at the pay shed and then we went to the pit canteen for a pot of tea and two of the biggest ham sandwiches you have ever seen. We ate one between us and the other went in his snap tin and he winked at me. 'There's double ham in that one — Mary's sent it for your mum and sisters to share.'

Everyone jumped on the buses provided by the pit and off we went to Barnsley, Christmas shopping. It was a fantastic few hours and we went home on the normal bus with a Christmas tree, a turkey and all manner of things. He'd even bought Mum the latest electric washer (I think it was a twin-tub machine) which was delivered at 11.30 that night, when I was fast asleep.

Telling this story reminded me of another that happened about forty years ago. Because I was from Barnsley and my fore-bears were either miners or farmers (apart from one who was the designer and architect for Sheffield's railway station) I was always getting ribbed about how easy a coal miner's job was. This prompted me to arrange a Sunday morning trip down Barrow Main colliery near Worsbrough village, courtesy of a friend of mine, Brian Kingston, who was the training officer there. There were, I think, ten of us in all including a top CID man and we were quickly kitted out with helmets, lamps and shin pads. We then entered the cage that took us down to the pit bottom. On the descent nobody spoke. I had to smile because they were terrified already. It was a fair walk to the coalface and my mate Rick banged his head on a girder. Poor Rick was suffering a hangover at the time, which made it even worse, and he cursed like a good 'un. When we got to the coalface Brian told us to crawl through the narrow gap, about two foot high, and follow him, which we did. After a short distance we stopped and, as told, we switched off our lamps. The blackness was unreal. It was total darkness.

'Above you, gentlemen, are millions of tons of rock and coal which is only supported by wooden or steel chocks and I am now going to release one of them.' Crack! We thought the roof would cave in – the noise was deafening and the impact it had on us was one of sheer terror. One of our party screamed out loud and everyone was cursing.

'For God's sake, Brian, get us out of here,' we shouted as we fumbled to switch our lamps back on. We were crawling on our hands and knees in a line, Brian in front and me at the back. It was a long crawl to the tailgate at the other side of the face, but within a minute it was obvious from the smell that one of our party had had an accident in his pants, but nobody admitted it. Eventually we got back to the pit bottom and the cage. It was the end of the shift and everyone was fighting to get in the cage. First to get into it was the first to get out of the pit. The cage limit was forty but I counted seventy-three in the first one — forty going down and sometimes eighty going up. My mate Ray once told me that they were like sardines in a can, so eager were they to get out. After a shower we went to the canteen and our top CID man asked to meet the manager. He thanked Brian and the manager for allowing us down and his parting words were, 'That was an eye-opener for us all and we thought we were going to die down there. If any of your men commit a crime in Sheffield, including murder, I'll guarantee them bail, they deserve it.'

Our other pre-Christmas duty was called Turkey Patrol, another name for an extra crime car. Poor old Billy Burglar needed extra cash for Christmas just like the rest of us and, like the steelworkers and the miners, he had to work extra hours to get it. He'd worked out that everyone was so busy near Christmas, including the police, that they wouldn't have time to bother with the likes of him and he was rubbing his hands with glee at the thought of rich pickings. How wrong he was. We wanted to spoil his Christmas this year and the bosses had given us a plainclothes car to help us in our endeavours.

The duty was called Turkey Patrol because tens of thousands of turkeys were hung up in and outside butchers' shops all over the city, waiting to be gobbled up on Christmas Day. For this reason we gave special or extra attention to these premises, along with off-licences, which provided a port or whisky after the turkey had been eaten. On this particular night I had a police constable working with me who had about three years' service and, as I was the driver, his job was to be sharp-eyed and to look out for Burglar Bill. We were at liberty to work anywhere in the division and check the areas that we thought might be the most vulnerable. I made my way towards the Firth Park area but we didn't spot anything of interest. A tour around Tinsley also proved negative. The Cliffe, for a change, was quiet, so I drove towards the city, along Brightside Lane, looking up every side street that we passed whilst checking for any movement that might be of a nefarious nature. Nothing. Further along Brightside Lane I turned left into Stevenson Road and wondered how the old man with the pram full of coal – and his granddaughter – were going on, but something was niggling me and, at the end of the road, I turned the car round and headed back. 'What's tha up to?' asked Geoff.

'Not sure yet but why was that Bedford van parked up

near Ropers Yard back on Brightside Lane? I've never seen one there before.'

'I've no idea, I didn't even see it,' he replied.

I made my way back and parked up outside the Midland pub just off Newhall Road where we had a good view of the van. I switched off the lights and lit a fag.

'Why are we waiting, there's no one in it?'

'That's why I'm waiting. The back windows are blacked out. It's just a hunch. We'll give it half an hour,' I replied. After forty minutes I was still niggled but couldn't put a finger on why, and in those days you couldn't check the registration number for an owner like you can today. Geoff wanted to move on and as he quite rightly said it could have broken down and be there all night. Something was still telling me to wait. A few minutes later I thought I saw the van move up and down a bit and nudged Geoff, who was nodding off.

'You were right, I saw it move then. I'll check,' and before I could stop him he was out of the car and off to the van. If there were two of you working together it was only right that you took a prisoner on an alternate basis and I'd nabbed a shop-breaker the night before. Less than five minutes later Geoff was back at our car.

'Well, what's what, is he okay?'

'Yes, he's okay, just took his dog for a walk, that's all. What a waste of time.'

'What's in the van?'

'Cardboard boxes, he delivers mail order stuff.'

'Where does he live?'

'Rawmarsh.' At this reply I just went berserk.

'A man from Rawmarsh – ten miles away – walking his dog for an hour at one in the morning and a van full of boxes, and you think he's okay and all we've done is waste time. I don't think so! Sit tight, we're off.'

'Where to?' Geoff asked.

'To catch a lying pillock who's just driven off, that's where.'

The car engine was screaming as I chased after him down Brightside Lane, Meadowhall Road and Meadow Bank. He obviously thought he'd got away with it, as he took the direct route towards home – any other route and we would have lost him. As I pulled him in, the look on his face told me I was right and he knew the game was up. I was still boiling over. 'Open the van doors.' He opened a side door, which was why we couldn't see him putting the imaginary dog in when we saw the van bounce. 'Back doors as well.' The van was full of cardboard boxes of various sizes and several large and empty hessian sacks. I examined the boxes with the aid of my torch. Several were marked 'Grattans', a firm I was aware of because my mum was an agent for them. Mrs Smith of Falmouth, Mr Brown of Cardiff, Mr McNee of Edinburgh, the boxes said. There were addresses all over the British Isles and the boxes were all open. 'Father Christmas has a lot of miles to cover to deliver all this lot and in an old van as well. Where are they from?' He didn't answer and so I said to Geoff, 'Sit with him, don't speak and we'll go back to where we first saw him. I'll follow you.'

We pulled in where he'd been parked and I decided to have a look around while Geoff held on to him. I walked up a narrow path which only brought me to a mass of railway lines, containing empty carriages and wagons full of coal and iron scrap. Not from here then. And then it dawned on me, it *was* from here because there were also box vans there, but you couldn't see into them. I went back to the van.

'Now I know where Father Christmas does his shopping,' I said. I arrested him under caution and told him we were fetching the railway police. His reply was rather odd, I thought.

'They'll be chuffed, they've been after me for years.' When the railway police arrived they couldn't believe their luck, there was even a list in his van. Shoes, brown brogue, size ten, black, size six and so on. The list was endless: shoes, jumpers, toys, jewellery, perfume, all with ticks at the side and all in his van. He stole to order. He had no previous convictions so apparently had never had his fingerprints taken, but when they were checked he was wanted for jobs on railway sidings all over the country and over several years, including mail bags containing postal orders. He was on the

British Rail top three most wanted list and it cleared up a lot of countrywide theft for them. His knowledge of the railway system had been gleaned over the years that he'd worked for them and he knew which carriage held what, so he could steal whatever you wanted, from anywhere in the country.

He missed his Christmas dinner for the next five years whilst we later received a nice commendation from the Chief Constable of British Rail, for our observational skills and diligence.

After a late snap-time we made our way through Darnall and the Manor. It would be daylight in thirty minutes so all respectable burglars should be in bed by then. The radio sprang to life. 'Is any mobile near to Harborough Avenue? A six-year-old boy has rung 999 to say that his step-dad has beaten up his mother. He's been told to wait in the tele-phone kiosk until someone gets there.' We were only 300 yards away and even though we were the crime car we said that we'd attend the incident. Domestics were often just family squabbles and easily sorted but a six-year-old dialling 999 was something else. The poor little thing was in the kiosk and crying. He was in his pyjamas but had no shoes on so I picked him up and walked to our car while at the same time trying to pacify the lad, but he just kept saying, 'Me dad's hitting me mam.'

The front door of the house was open and a couple of neighbours were standing nearby. They knew little Jack and he knew them so one of the ladies took him to her house out of the way. 'He's a nasty piece of work, mate. He's turned up tonight after two years and hammered her,' explained a chap from across the road. I walked down the hallway and into the lounge. To my right was a thin young woman, covered in blood from her nose and mouth. Her eyes and lips were badly bruised and a broken tooth was on the floor near to where she lay. On the left was the woman beater, about forty years of age, 5' 10" tall and heavily built.

'I hope that you are proud of what you've done to her,' I said.

'F*** off. I hate coppers,' was the pleasant reply and he swung his right leg at my groin. Luckily, he only got the inside of my leg, as I stepped back. I looked again at the woman. 'Do you want this man in your house or shall I eject him?'

'I thought he'd gone two years ago, but he's just out of prison for beating me up before. Please chuck him out.'

'Martyn, he's got a knife,' Geoff shouted. Sure enough, in his right hand was an old-fashioned steel carving knife with an eight-inch blade. It looked bigger as it flashed past my nose end and he made several attempts to slash me up. In front of me was an aluminium Formica-topped kitchen table. I picked it up and, table top facing him, I ran at him and squashed him up against the wall. He dropped the knife as the table had winded him. 'Geoff, open that front door and the back door of the police car. I'm bringing him out. Little Jack's okay, love, he's across the road being looked after by a neighbour.'

As I grabbed hold of him he somehow managed to head-butt me in the mouth and also kicked his wife in the stomach. I didn't retaliate, but dragged him to our car, parked near the front door, where Geoff had the cuffs waiting and we bundled him in and drove off. I didn't speak on the way to the nick. I was thinking about poor little Jack and his battered mother. What a thing for a child to witness. Another of my teeth had gone and my lips felt like heavy-duty tyres. I was getting uglier by the day. Back at the nick we released him from his handcuffs and as we did so he kicked Geoff in the groin and swung at me again.

I'd stood enough now and I'll leave it to your imagination as to what happened next. Suffice it to say that summary justice was administered on a man-to-man basis. A while later Mr Brute, the woman beater, who had thirteen convictions for violence, was sent back to prison for six years.

Woolworths was busy, which was not surprising as it was Christmas Eve. I was on afternoon shift and, when I got back from Sheffield, I was just in time to pick up the normal police car at 3 pm. With the gaffer's permission I went to see Jack at his house. All the lads on our shift had been impressed by little Jack's bravery, running to the phone in the middle of the night and then knowing how to use it at the age of six. We'd all chipped in to buy him a toy police car for Christmas. When I pulled up at the house the neighbours' curtains were twitching and little Jack was playing on the pavement with a pal. His mum came out looking better than when I last saw her and she started to cry when I gave her the parcel. Little Jack was looking at the police car with three little pals. 'Come on, you four, jump in. I'll give you a ride.' Their little faces were beaming, especially when the blue light came on.

It gave me a nice warm feeling when I dropped them off and shouted, 'Happy Christmas.' The neighbours had seen the kids in the car and, as I drove away, they were all waving and shouted, 'Happy Christmas' to me as I departed.

We received a nice letter from Jack's mum over Christmas. He loved the car and she thanked the entire shift for being kind.

I never saw them again and Little Jack will now be Big Jack but I'm sure he'll have turned out okay.

CHAPTER SEVENTEEN

Nowt as Queer as Folk

I've said it before and I'll say it again: a policeman can never tell from one minute to the next what he'll have to deal with. It could vary tremendously and you had to be constantly on your toes in case the next job you came across was something that you'd never experienced before. You learnt something new every day and filed that experience in your memory box, just in case you encountered it again.

Along with the Ambulance and Fire Service we were usually the first to the scene of an incident and, in consequence, often had to deal with horrendous situations and adapt our actions accordingly ... and sometimes in odd ways.

I was on nights once on Attercliffe Common when I came across a young man in a collapsed condition lying on the pavement, with a hypodermic syringe in his hand. We had no radios in those days and the phone in the kiosk at the top of Weedon Street wasn't working so I couldn't call for help. I knew that by the time I'd gone and got assistance it would be too late anyway and so decided to stay with him in his dying moments.

He was saying something to me which, at first, I couldn't catch. Then he spoke again, very quietly.

'Is that you, Mam?' I was about to say, 'No, lad,' when he spoke again. 'Is that you, Mam?'

'Yes, son, it is. I'm here,' I replied.

'Have I been a bad son, Mam?'

'Of course not, love, you've been a very good son.'

'Stroke my forehead, Mam, like you used to do when I was little.'

I lifted his head and cradled him in my arms while I stroked his forehead, hoping that I'd got it right. His voice was getting weaker as he spoke again and I had to put my ear to his mouth in order to hear him.

'Does my dad love me like you do, Mam?'

'He does love you, son, just like I do – don't worry, everything is all right, love, you just rest, son.'

'I'm sorry, Mam, I love ...' And with that his voice tailed off and his head lolled to one side and he was gone. While I was still kneeling on the pavement with his head resting in the crook of my left arm I managed to light a fag and just knelt there for a few minutes with tears streaming down my cheeks. What a waste of a life.

Drugs were fairly new to us then and they had just ruined a whole family for the sake of some greedy bastard making a few quid.

It was this sort of experience that taught you always to expect the unexpected. I never thought that one day I would play mother to a dying man, but I was glad he didn't die on his own, poor lad. I never told the lads at the nick that I'd cried but for some reason I'm telling you. If compassion means that I'm unmanly then so be it.

New experience number two happened when I was on the car beat at Firth Park, working 7 am to 3 pm. The morning had been fairly quiet and at about 11.15 I went back to the little sub-station for my snap and a cuppa. Halfway through my snap there was a knock on the door and on opening it I was met with a man dressed in scruffy overalls, wellies and a flat cap.

'Come in,' I said. 'How can I help you?' I could see that he was shaking and, although his mouth kept opening and closing, nothing coherent was coming out. He was in shock. 'Calm yourself down and then tell me what the problem is.' I made him a cuppa and put plenty of sugar in it in order to bring him round a bit. I sat him down. He wasn't deaf or dumb but he was stuttering. After a while his speech began to get more normal.

'I'm the ratcatcher for this area,' he stuttered.

'And?' I asked gently.

'There was a report of a lot of rats seen near a sewer pipe down the road.'

'So why are you here and so upset?'

'I went to investigate and there's a dead body in the sewer pipe.'

I informed the office sergeant at Attercliffe and told him that I'd ring him again later and then followed the man down to the spot concerned. The rat man had told me to bring a torch and we both clambered down the embankment to where I could see a large concrete pipe, maybe four foot in diameter, running in a horizontal position and going under the road above us. From the pipe came a small but steady stream of water which, having left the pipe, created a rivulet through the undergrowth.

I shone the torch into the pipe and peered in, looking for the body, but all I could see were several rats scurrying about.

'Where's the body, mate?' I asked.

'Further up there. We'll have to crawl. Follow me.'

'Great,' I thought, 'crawling up a rat-infested sewer is all I need.'

The rat man passed me some long rubber gloves and we were off into the dark. Rats were squealing everywhere. After about fifteen yards the rat man stopped and stood upright. We were now in a similar pipe but this one was vertical and, as I looked upwards with the torch, I could see that it was encased in a square red-brick structure. Because of the curve of the pipe there were four small ledges in each corner, shaped a bit like a triangle. Above this was an iron cover with a lever on it, which meant that we were in some sort of inspection hatch that could be opened from above.

'I can't see a body yet,' I said to the rat man.

'It's up there on that ledge,' he replied.

We both looked up and he pointed his torch into one of the corners of the chamber. I could see something but couldn't make out what, so I climbed a couple of rungs of the ladder that was set into the pipe and there it was. The body was in a crouched position on the ledge, with 'girlie books' lying in front of it.

New experience number two now came into play. It was a body all right, or rather what was left of one – it was, in the main, skeletal. The right arm, which was bare of clothing and raised into the air, had only a small amount of black flesh on it near to the wrist. There was some sort of ligature tied to the wrist, which passed over an iron bar above the body and, from there, it was wrapped around the neck. I'd never seen anything like this before and never since. I was well aware that this was probably a crime scene so I didn't go any nearer. We retraced our steps and I told the rat man to wait at the entrance to the sewer and not to let anyone in. I couldn't imagine anyone in their right mind wanting to but

I had to be sure and it gave him something to do whilst I went to summon help. Radio reception was non-existent so I called for help from a nearby pub. I could have murdered a pint but declined the landlord's kind offer.

The cavalry arrived in the form of the CID along with the police photographer and it was obviously a new experience for them as well as for me. It was certainly a puzzler. It was now a job for the CID and a few of us uniform officers were asked to sift through the muddy waters of the rivulet after it left the sewer. We were told to look for anything that might be of interest to the inquiry.

The body had obviously been there for some time and it was my understanding that, when it rained heavily, both pipes would contain volumes of surface water which would have washed any evidence away. As a result of this nothing was found and we were sent back to normal duties.

The day after, it was established that the body was male and he had been reported missing from home about nine months previously. Professor Alan Usher, the well-respected pathologist, said that the man had died of accidental asphyxiation whilst indulging in some form of sexual activity and, although I didn't see it at the time I first saw the body, he had a length of rubber pipe in his anus; and he was wearing a short, green lady's nightie. This was the first case of its kind to be seen in Sheffield. No one else was involved and the incident was classed as accidental death.

These unusual situations are rare but become part of a policeman's way of life. Some are funny, some are sad, and you would be amazed at some of the things people get up to.

I was on foot patrol one night at Darnall and all was quiet. One of the lads was taking four hours off to have an early start to his annual leave and I was taking over his motorbike beat at 3 am. It was a lovely summer's night. As I walked down Staniforth Road, I could hear Brown Bailey's drop hammer in the distance. It was about 1 am and I decided to spend twenty minutes or so watching the Co-op on Ribston Road. It had been broken into a few weeks before by removing the slates off the roof and a large amount of cigarettes had been stolen; you never know, the culprits might come back for more. The Co-op was on a corner, so I positioned myself in some shadows where I could see it from all angles and waited.

After about fifteen minutes I could hear a noise. There was a tap, tap and then nothing. I knew every noise on my patch but this one sounded like someone hitting a chisel with a hammer, so I looked at the Co-op roof, but there was no one on it. A minute or two later I heard it again – tap, tap – and I realised that the noise was coming from somewhere down the road, but nearby. I tiptoed towards it and waited again. Tap, tap. I was near to it now. Again, tap, tap – I was at a wooden gate that led to the rear yard of some terraced houses and from the light of an open doorway I could see a man on his hands and knees with a hammer and a chisel. I scratched my head and wondered what he was up to. Tap, tap again. I could see that he was hitting the tarmac in the yard. At that time in the morning he was bound to be up to no good. He couldn't get away though since at the other end of the yard was the large gable end of Bone Cravens Works. He was mine.

I carefully lifted the latch on the gate in order to surprise him but, as it opened, it creaked and he saw me. 'Stand where you are, it's the police – what's tha up to?' I was near him now and keeping an eye on the hammer.

'Bugger off, it's nowt to do wi' thee.'

I grabbed the hammer and asked him again, 'As you can see, I'm the police. What's tha up to?' His attitude altered.

'Come on in.'

We both went into the house and he sat at the kitchen table and indicated to me to do the same.

'If tha must know, me pet budgie's died and I'm trying to bury it before t'kids get up for school. They'll be upset an' all.' And he promptly burst into tears. There on the table was a dead budgie wrapped in cotton wool and tissue paper. I wanted to laugh but daren't, he was so upset. None of the thousands of houses around me had any garden, so I suppose he had no option but to bury it in the yard. 'You'll feel better when you've had a cup of tea,' I said to him, hopefully.

'Good idea, will you have one?'

'That would be nice, thanks.'

After a chat about budgies and having drunk my tea, I bade him goodnight and off I went. I wrote in my pocket book later: 'No burglars tonight but laid a budgie to rest.'

I made my way back to the nick and told the lads the story, which had them laughing. After eating my cold fish sandwiches, which I loved, and my banana, I picked up the motorbike ready for off.

'See you, tweetie-pie,' shouted one of the lads. I gave him the signal made famous at the Battle of Agincourt, way before Mr Churchill's time – and rode away.

Less than five minutes later the radio crackled into life: 'Attend such and such an address, where an ambulance has been called to an unknown incident.' When you were on a mobile beat you would often get four or five incidents per shift to deal with and they could be anything from someone with a broken leg to a suicide or murder. By a strange coincidence I was riding up the road concerned and on checking the door numbers I could see that I was only about fifty yards from the house. I could hear the birds singing, which heralded dawn breaking. I took off my crash helmet and placed it on the bike seat and walked to the front door of the terraced house. A knock on the open door caused a large woman in a dressing gown and slippers to appear. Her hair was in those big round curlers and her face was like thunder. She was awesome. Her hands were on her hips and she reminded me of a sumo wrestler. The lady meant business. Another new experience was about to come my way.

Pointing into the house, she shouted, 'Get in there, the dirty bastard's in the kitchen.'

'Who do you think you're talking to?' I replied, indignantly.

'You get in the kitchen, didn't they tell you why I'd rung?'

It suddenly dawned on me that she thought I was the ambulance man because I wasn't wearing a helmet. I'd beaten them to it so I went into the kitchen, followed by Miss World. The sight that met me was one that I'll never forget.

As I passed through the kitchen doorway I could see a man aged about fifty. He was standing upright but the top half of his body was bent forward at 90 degrees and his outstretched hands and arms were resting on his knees as though he needed to support himself. As I entered he was looking up at me from this odd position and with a very silly half-grin on his face he said, 'Good morning.'

I returned the greeting and at the same time saw that his pyjama bottoms were round his ankles, near to where a couple of girlie magazines lay open on the floor.

'I'll give you good morning,' said Miss World as she came past me and promptly started slapping his face as hard as she could, whilst at the same time shouting, 'Dirty bastard.'

She'd pushed by me and I could see now what the problem was. Behind the man was an old-fashioned mangle with two rollers, set on a cast iron frame. These rollers were operated by a handle which was fastened to a frame at the top. The vertical handle was in the downwards position towards the floor; the small handle for turning the mangle, which projected at 90 degrees in the horizontal position, was nowhere to be seen. I thought I knew where the handle was hiding and, for once, I was speechless.

Why is it that we all want to laugh when we're not supposed to? If a man hits his thumb with a hammer or drops it on his toes it's instinctive, for some reason, to laugh. I'd heard the expression 'He's on a roll' before but knew that it had a different connotation in the scene that was set out before me. I just could not help sniggering and every time his wife clipped him I did everything I could to try not to laugh out loud. Tears were rolling down my cheeks. Trying to tell yourself not to laugh only makes it worse and, thankfully, at this point two ambulance men ran into the house and saw what I had seen a few minutes earlier. The mangle man looked very sheepish and the ambulance men were scratching their heads and I could see that they were also trying not to laugh.

I took them both outside for a discussion on what to do next and one of them said, without realising the funny side, 'We'll have to get to the bottom of this.' That set us off. My sides were aching with laughter and, for a few minutes, all three of us totally lost control.

We were back inside the house in time to see his wife clip him yet again. Something had to be done before she killed him. We looked at the mechanism of the mangle, but the only way to release the handle, which was attached to the long cast iron piece, was with a screwdriver, but we couldn't get to the screw because of the iron frame. Short of spinning the man round like the hands on a clock, there was nothing we could do.

'That's it,' I thought, 'the next step is to call for the fire brigade. They'll have to cut the mangle up in order to release him.' I phoned the office sergeant from the bike radio and outlined the situation and asked that the fire brigade attend with as little fuss as possible. I was still shaking my head in disbelief at what I had seen.

When Miss World had gone to bed earlier, leaving Mr Mangle to his own devices, so to speak, little did she think that she would wake up to such a scene, and imagine his embarrassment at having to shout for her because of his predicament. No wonder she was mad at him.

I thought I could hear a siren and sure enough it was getting nearer. The message must not have been properly passed on because, when they arrived, the men jumped out and started to unroll a fire hose. 'He's got problems enough as it is without a hosepipe. All we need is cutting gear,' I said and went back into the house. The next minute all the firemen rushed into the house. Hugh, Pugh, Barnie, McGrew, Cuthbert

Dibble and Grub – they ran in just like the characters in the children's programme *Camberwick Green*. They each in turn saw what I and the ambulance lads had seen earlier and doubled up in silent laughter.

A few minutes later, with the aid of a hacksaw, the mangle was dismantled. The short turning handle, however, was still in situ and the hospital would have to release that. Mr Mangle wasn't in pain apart from sore ears where his wife had given him a few clips and he went to hospital on a stretcher, lying face down.

You just can't help but laugh even though you shouldn't. We all agreed that it was a new experience for us and one of the firemen had the last word when he said of Mr Mangle, 'He just couldn't handle it!'

No one had committed a criminal offence and so that was the end of the matter. I told you. There's nowt as queer as folk.

CHAPTER EIGHTEEN

In Trouble at Home

When serving a summons or executing a warrant for someone's arrest you got various reactions. On this particular occasion I'd gone to a house in Tinsley to arrest someone wanted on warrant for non-payment of a fine. I knocked on the door, which was answered by a gorilla. He was a big mean-looking guy and when I told him that I was arresting him he said, 'You're not taking me anywhere, mate, I'm a black belt in karate.' A lot of people have told me this over the years but I learnt that, for most, such comments were all mouth and trousers. In reality such people were pussycats to deal with. This one, however, was the exception, but I wasn't to know that until he'd knocked me to the ground for the third time. He was now coming in for the killer punch and I realised that it was my last chance to stop him. I managed to avoid the blow as he came to me on the floor and at the same time I swung an almighty punch at him with my right fist. There was a piercing scream followed by 'What are you doing? Are you trying to kill me?' I jumped up, startled.

I wasn't the only one to be startled. Standing in front of me was Christine, my wife. She was in her nightclothes and holding the right side of her face, which was swelling up. 'What do you think you are doing?' At that point I realised that it was all a dream and that I'd finished work an hour before (having been on nights) and gone straight to bed. I always used to sleep on my back with Christine on my left. Luckily the blow had travelled from my right side and across my chest and at that point the blow couldn't travel any further distance and it just caught her on the right cheekbone.

She was not pleased at all, even after I explained. 'It was an accident, I'm sorry, I was dreaming,' I said.

'It's me that's sorry, for marrying you.' Her cheek puffed up a bit but nothing was broken. Fancy waking up with your husband having hit you, albeit in his sleep. I was under the covers now. I'm far from being a cruel man but I could see the funny side of it and, as usual, I had to laugh – but under the covers! The more I said sorry the worse it got and the words 'divorce', 'suitcase' and 'back to my mum's' were mentioned several times.

I had to make amends somehow so I got up and offered to

take her to Ron's Café at Tinsley for breakfast, but that went down like a lead balloon. We both loved breakfast at Ron's but not today, and as I went back to bed I knew I was in bother. Funny things, women – I resigned myself to a bad day.

When I got up at about 4 pm Christine had calmed down a bit and we had tea with Richard and Sally, our children, who were just toddlers then. It must have shook her up a bit but she was okay really. I still had to make amends.

At about 7.15 pm the phone rang and I answered it. It was a male voice speaking in very hushed tones.

'Martyn, is that you?'

'Yes, who's that?' It was Brian, the landlord of the Mason's Arms, my local, at Thorpe Hesley.

'What's up wi' you? I can hardly hear you.'

'I opened up at seven o'clock and this great big chap came in and asked for you.'

'Who is it?' I asked.

'I don't know, I'm hiding behind the bar, terrified. He's got a pint and he's prowling round the pub.'

'I'll be down in a bit.'

When I got to the Mason's the lights were on and I crept in the darkness to the side window and looked in. There prowling about with a face like thunder was Big Ian. Brian was right, he was about 6′ 5″ and solid muscle. I'd locked him up about three years earlier for the theft of a lorry containing a load of new tyres, for which he got six months in prison. During the interview he was pacing about angrily and I discovered that he couldn't read or write, not even his own name. He had a massive chip on his shoulder as a result of this and, on his release, I visited his mum's house in Attercliffe and started to teach him to read and write. He was understandably embarrassed, but, after a year, he was doing well and I made him go to night classes. His anger abated and his confidence grew. I instilled it into him that if he got into bother he must come and see me.

I walked into the pub, which was empty apart from Ian, and all I could see of the landlord was the top of his head behind the bar. Ian saw me and shook my hand so hard that I thought it would fall off.

'Mr Johnson, the police have done me in Derbyshire.'

'What for?' I asked.

'They said I went through the lights on red, but they were on amber. You're the only man in the world that I trust – if you tell me to plead guilty that's what I'll do.'

At this point in walked another Brian, my mate, and as Ian and I walked past him he pretended to trip me up and laughed. I heard a whooshing noise and turned to see Brian stuck on the ceiling, being held up there with just Ian's right arm.

'You even think about touching Mr Johnson and I'll kill you.' And looking at me Ian then said, 'Can I throw him through the window?'

'No! He's my mate, Ian, put him down.'

Both Brians were at the bar and shaking like rabid dogs. Ian and I sat down for a chat.

'I haven't seen you for a while, are you still down The Cliffe?'

'No, I live with a bird in Derbyshire and work on the bins,' he replied.

'How did you find me?'

'You once mentioned the Mason's Arms and I knew that you lived in Thorpe Hesley.'

'You've come a long way to ask me that question, Ian.'

'That's because I only trust you.'

'How did you get here?'

He looked at the floor and said, 'I borrowed a car and put some petrol in it for him.'

'Is he a mate?' I asked – even though I thought I knew what the answer would be.

'No, I don't know him but he'll have it back in an hour.'

'Are you still disqualified from driving, Ian?'

'Yes, Mr Johnson. But I had to see you, you'll tell me what to do.'

'I think you'd better plead guilty, Ian. Let me get a pint.' I went to the bar and heard him shout, 'Thanks, Mr Johnson,' and he was gone. What a silly thing to do, how the hell could you worry about going through traffic lights at red when you've just 'borrowed' a car, are driving while disqualified and with no insurance. It would have been a waste of time ringing the police – he wasn't daft, he'd have parked away from the pub so that no one knew what he was driving and he'd have gone back to somewhere in Derbyshire, via Timbuktu knowing Ian, to avoid being caught. I shook my head – a funny thing, trust. What a day so far: I was walking on eggshells with my wife and then Ian doing something stupid. I thought at the time that it would be a good job when I got to work and out of the way.

The cold fish and tomato sauce sandwiches were packed up along with my usual banana and I was ready for the night shift. Christine was okay now and we had a laugh about it. We kissed goodnight and she told me to be careful as she always did. Even when we were courting she insisted on walking me to the bus stop when I was on nights and giving me a little peck on the cheek before I boarded the bus. It was embarrassing getting on a bus full of drunks but they all thought better of saying anything. I loved her for it and always have.

It was nice to be at work and it wasn't too cold even though winter time was only about a month away. I worked the beat, checking the shops to make sure that they were secure and occasionally standing in a doorway watching for any signs of criminal activity. All was quiet, which suited me after the day's events, and I was looking forward to snap-time. The radio was also quiet apart from a report that someone had seen a man waving a gun about in the Wicker a couple of miles away. I was making my way back to the nick for my break when a car pulled up.

'I've just seen a man on the roof of Burton's Buildings at the bottom of Staniforth Road.'

The last time I'd been there was when a man was not getting his own way when claiming benefits from the DHSS, whose offices were housed in the buildings. A PC had attended but then asked for assistance – and quickly. Four of us arrived there almost together and ran upstairs to the office, which had a wooden floor. Inside were a lot of tubular steel chairs, bolted to the floor in rows of ten. Mr Unhappy Man had vented his anger on the office staff and then ripped a row of chairs up out of the floor. People were terrified but couldn't get past him as he swung the chairs around his head.

We assessed the scene and it was decided that four of us would rush him while the fifth got the cuffs ready to restrain him and thus prevent any more damage. We drew him to an area of floor which had less broken glass on it than other areas and, on the count of three, we went in – rugby style. We decided earlier who was to grab which limb and mine was one of his arms, which happened to be wielding the chairs. It worked a treat and he was on the floor in seconds but still thrashing about. My mate Ken was holding a leg and I saw him shoot across the room, still holding the leg. Ken's face was a picture of horror until he realised that the leg he was holding was false! We all had a laugh at Ken later and the man was charged with criminal damage and assault on the staff.

Back to the job in hand. As I approached the three-storey building, I looked up but couldn't see any sign of anyone. It was about 3 am and I saw a man standing outside the phone box near to Burton's Buildings. 'What are you doing at this time of the morning?'

'Waiting for a taxi home,' he casually replied. He looked okay to me but then said, 'Are you looking for a man on a roof?'

'Yes, I am.'

'I don't know what he's up to but I've just seen him about three minutes since.' He pointed to the roof area. I knew the property well as we checked it every night and I knew that the only way up was by a fire escape ladder at the back of the premises. I crept round the back and to the ladder which went up three storeys to the roof. Now climbing and heights are not my strong point (I could get dizzy with two pairs of socks on) but slowly and very quietly I got to the top. I was just on the point of looking over the parapet when I was met by a man crouched down and pointing a silvery-looking gun towards me.

He was holding the gun, which was similar to a Beretta pistol but bigger, in both hands (very professional) about two feet from my face and then he spoke: 'F*** off. The first copper to come up here gets a bullet.' I was shaking as I climbed back down and wished that my trousers were brown and not blue. My bad day was getting worse.

I knew that this was his only way down so I stood at the side of the entry while I used the radio to ask for assistance. There were no standby firearm units or trained negotiators in those days and no roads were closed either, we just had to deal with it. Assistance turned up in the form of my mate PC Brian Ragg (we always called him Wing Commander Ragg simply because the tips of his collar never ever lay flat and were always turned up over his tunic so looked as though they were just about to take off). He arrived on his motorbike and I related the story to him and he said, 'I'll bet it's that bloke who was waving a gun about in the Wicker a couple of hours ago.' I thought this was a good bit of deduction and that he was probably right.

Brian went to the front of the building to try and draw the man's attention whilst I went to go up the fire escape again. I was part way up it when a house brick whistled past my left lughole.

'I'll kill you, you bastard, if you come near me and I've got a gun to do it with.' I scrambled back down the ladder to the floor a lot quicker than when I went up and as I stood there looking up into the darkness above I was pelted with more bits of masonry. I had no option but to back off. At the same time something heavy (which turned out to be a chimney cowl) hit me on the right hand. I was in agony and later found out that I'd got a broken knuckle and two smaller bones chipped. I retreated back to the end of the alleyway and as I did so the police inspector and some of the lads turned up. The man was trapped up there but we had to somehow get him down.

The boss decided to send for the fire brigade who had a turntable ladder and also asked for a police dog and handler, of which there were only a few in those days. The fire crew arrived with a fairly young divisional officer and they were followed by the police dog handler. The dog and handler, myself and another PC went up on the hydraulic ladder which was extremely scary in itself. Someone had distracted Al Capone and, when we got to roof level, he was at the other side of the building.

What a nightmare. The dog wouldn't jump on to the roof before us and by now laddo was getting nearer and pointing his gun and shouting, 'The first one that comes gets it.' We were in big trouble until the handler picked up the dog and threw him onto the roof and this meant that we could follow. From his training the dog knew to grab the man's arm just above the hand in which he was carrying the gun, enabling the rest of us to quickly restrain him. Then we were all lowered to the floor. At that point I discovered that the gun was, in fact, a chrome-plated cigarette lighter in the form of an automatic pistol, but you would not have been able to tell the difference between that and a real one, even in day-light. When coupled with the sighting of a man waving a gun in the Wicker the same night and Al Capone threatening to shoot us, it wasn't surprising that we thought it was real.

I told him that he was under arrest and he replied, 'I hate you, you bastard, I wish that brick had killed you and your kids as well,' and then he spat in my face. He'd already broken my hand so all I could do was to push him towards the wall with my left hand.

'You've just assaulted that man! I want to make a complaint.' It was the young divisional fire officer and everyone looked at him in amazement, including the firemen. Our inspector came forward at this point and said, 'My officer has been threatened with a gun and pelted with rocks, resulting in a broken hand. This lunatic wishes him and his children dead and he has been spat upon, and you want to complain about a gentle push made by him?' The inspector continued: 'Thank you for your assistance here tonight, now you concentrate on your job and we'll concentrate on ours – catching criminals.' What a moment. Everyone at the scene, including the firemen, clapped.

The comments made by the fire officer were more a topic of conversation than the job itself and it was the only time in our collective memories that anything like that had happened. We had too much respect for each other's jobs to fall out, especially over something as petty as a push.

When I got home from work that morning I gave the kids, who were asleep in bed, a kiss. After all, I could easily have been killed with the house bricks or chimney cowl that night.

Christine's face was fine and when the kids woke we went to Ron's Café at Tinsley for breakfast. The kids loved it there and, when Sally was fifteen, we asked what she would like for her birthday and she asked to go to Ron's Café before school as a birthday treat. Ron and Margaret always made a fuss over Sally, Richard and toddler Paul, as did the customers. Even today they still go to Ron's Café occasionally.

In those days you had a magistrates' court, quarter sessions which were held every three months and then the big one: Sheffield's assize court. Our man was sent to the quarter sessions court which could mete out a bigger sentence than the magistrates'. He pleaded guilty to attempting to break into the building on Attercliffe Road, attempting to steal and also assaulting yours truly. The circumstances of the case were outlined by the prosecution counsel and the defence's excuse was that he had drunk ten pints that night. The judge asked if he had any complaints or anything to say. From the dock he turned and looked at me and said to the judge, 'I have no complaints, sir, but I would like to apologise to PC Johnson for assaulting him and also saying what I did. I was lucky not to get a good hiding that night which I fully deserved.'

The judge commended us on our brave actions and sentenced laddo to twelve months' imprisonment suspended for two years, which meant that if he kept his nose clean then he would suffer no hardship at all.* It didn't make sense to me – the message to other criminals was quite simple: say that you have drunk ten pints of beer, go out with an imitation firearm, threaten the police with it then throw bricks at them and injure one whilst trying to break into a building in order to steal. Afterwards, if you apologise in court, all that will be forgiven. I was not pleased to say the least and it certainly didn't make our job any easier or bode well for the future.

Ah well. At least we did our job right.

---

*A full report of this incident headed 'I'll shoot the first copper', appeared in the Sheffield *Star* on 7 January 1974.

CHAPTER NINETEEN

If Only . . .

If only I'd been on another shift.
If only I'd been on a different beat.
If only I'd been on annual leave!

I'd started work at 7 am on this particular beat and I was whistling away. Would I have time for a pot of tea and a bacon buttie before I saw the kids across the busy main road on their way to school? The answer was yes but I would have to hurry. I walked briskly down the main road, passing several streets containing long rows of terraced houses on my left. As I got to the last one before the works I glanced to my left and near the top of the street I could see two or three men who appeared to be shouting, whilst I could see a fourth running, with a short ladder on his shoulder. They seemed to be in a panic. Within seconds I was at the scene and they were point-ing at one of the houses, which had clouds of smoke coming out of an open fanlight window on the ground floor.

'Has anyone phoned the fire brigade?' I shouted.

'We don't know, we saw the smoke from the works and we ran round.'

One of the men said that he would ring the fire brigade from the kiosk which was about fifty yards away at the bottom of the road, but it turned out someone had already rung them and they were on their way.

'Is anyone in the house?' I asked.

'Don't think so because we haven't heard or seen anyone.'

All this took a matter of seconds but by now neighbours, who had heard the shouting, were out in their nightclothes. It was only 7.20 am.

'Does anyone know who lives here?'

'A young couple with two toddlers. The man normally goes to work at 7 am,' replied one of the neighbours.

At this stage there was thick black smoke belching out of the windows. Where on earth were the firemen?

But of course they'd only just been called a minute before. The front bedroom window opened to reveal a young woman I had previously seen out shopping with two toddlers. What a nightmare. You couldn't see the bottom half of the house for smoke now as I put the ladder to the upstairs window and ran up it.

It wasn't high but high enough. The woman was standing in front of the window in her nightie.

'Pass the children out, I'll grab them,' I said.

'I can't find them,' she replied. The young woman was crying and hysterical.

'The house will go up any second, climb out NOW,' I shouted.

'I can't! I haven't any clothes on! Where are my kids?'

'Climb out! Climb out!' I was screaming at her now and managed to grab an arm through the thick smoke.

'The kids! The kids!' and she pulled away and I couldn't see her. The heat was unbearable and when I got to the ground I was shaking with sheer desperation. I felt totally and utterly helpless. Even though the fire brigade were now in attendance I knew it was too late. The house was engulfed in flames. The fire station was only a short distance away, but even so I don't know how they got there so quickly. The whole thing, from me at the bottom of the road to now, had taken five minutes maximum.

If only the workmen had seen it earlier.
If only I'd been there earlier.
If only neighbours had been awake earlier.
If only she'd opened the window earlier.
Such thoughts came into my mind.

All the emergency services were arriving now and yet you could have heard a pin drop, it was so quiet. We were all helpless and quite a few people, including me, were quietly crying. We all knew it was too late. Somehow we'd failed them and I felt sick to the pit of my stomach. I was sitting on the pavement when someone gave me a fag. I hadn't smoked for months but it tasted good. The fire was out now and it was my job to deal with the aftermath, which I knew would be horrible. I asked a fireman why the fire had been so ferocious and fast and he pointed to the downstairs ceiling. Polystyrene tiles were all the rage then and everyone had them, including me. The heat had melted them, which caused a flash fire and thick poisonous smoke. I found the two little ones just near the front bedroom window where I'd spoken to their mother, who was now lying on the floor under the window. Unfortunately they were beyond help but mum was just alive and she was whisked off to hospital, only to pass away a couple of weeks later. When found, mum was dressed. She must have managed to get some clothes.

I wanted to scream, 'Why? Why? Why?' to the man in heaven but it was too late. The feeling of guilt affected all of us. It was unimaginable.

If only she had found the children.
If only the tiles weren't polystyrene.
More sad thoughts.

It was concluded that the children had found some matches in the house and accidentally caused the fire.

It is not necessary to go into the horrendous details of what happened during the rest of the day, suffice it to say that relatives were contacted and we attended the mortuary. It was the most stressful thing I have ever dealt with and incidents like this stay with you for the rest of your life.

I went home late that night and my youngsters were fast asleep. I gently squeezed them and held their hands as I lay with them, sobbing. I wouldn't wish that day's events on my worst enemy. I felt that my guts had been ripped out and I would never be able to laugh again. People who have not experienced events like this can have no possible conception of the feelings encountered by ourselves and the fire service and I hope that they never will.

Several of our lads, firemen and I went to the funeral as a mark of respect and also to try and release some of our feelings. We were traumatised by the events but there were no counsellors then, you had to deal with it all by yourself. We'd all of us dealt with terrible things over the years and we were supposedly hardened – but not this time. Two little tots and their mum, it seemed so cruel and the words 'if only' have haunted me a million times ever since. There could be no final closure. Every time a fire is mentioned in the media it brings it all back to me, even after all these years.

*

My hobbies were and still are cricket, metal detecting and local history, so I immersed myself in them to try and forget. I was younger then and fitter and I travelled all over to go metal detecting. I met some great people, like Brian and Mary Booth from Warsop and Graham and Sylvia Carpenter from Dinnington. A lot of the stuff we found was given to local museums or schools for display purposes. Many years afterwards and after I'd left the job I was asked to do a live broadcast on *The Tony Capstick Show* on Radio Sheffield. The show lasted for about twenty minutes and we had a good laugh and enjoyed it. A few weeks later I was asked back again. The public had enjoyed it and wanted more. I had a twenty-minute slot with Cappo every two weeks, becoming known as Metal Detecting Martyn. The power of radio amazed me and, after the slot, people would ring in from as far afield as Leicester, Manchester and Hull asking for advice. Tony and I did many slots over two years or more and as a result many people were introduced to the hobby, including Ian Walker, my good buddy to this day.

Cappo was a fantastic guy, apart from his drinking, and we had loads of laughs together. We were true mates and, when he unfortunately died, I was privileged to be asked to do the eulogy at his funeral at Wentworth Church. My wife and I miss him greatly.

I'll not tell you her name but one of our fans was a lady who lived in a VERY big and famous house in Derbyshire.

During this time we did several outside broadcasts, having been invited to do so by farmers who wanted us to search their land. On one of these trips Cappo found two silver Roman coins, the jammy little bugger.

One day we decided to run a simple competition on the radio, the winner of which would join us and the Metal Detecting Club for a day out in the field. It was two weeks later when I was 'on' again and the winner was drawn from over 100 hopefuls. He joined us for a great day out in Lincolnshire. James was a nice guy and he luckily found a hammered silver coin for his trouble. He was over the moon. James had got the bug because two weeks later he phoned me after the programme and asked if I could help him as he wanted to buy a metal detector, so we arranged to meet up in a couple of days and go to a supplier in Scunthorpe.

On the way to Scunthorpe, we talked about metal detectors, fields, maps, research and getting permission to search. By the time we were near to Scunthorpe I'd had enough and changed the subject.

'Your accent sounds more southern than local,' I said to him.

'It will do, I've lived down south for many, many years but I was actually born in Sheffield.'

'Do you have a family?'

'Yes, the usual, a wife and two grown-up kids. You?'

'Yes, I've got three teenagers.'

'Did Tony say on the radio that you are an ex-Sheffield bobby?'

'That's right.'

'Where were you stationed?'

'Attercliffe, do you know it?'

'I have every respect for the police at Attercliffe.'

'That's nice to hear. Why is that then?' I asked.

He put his head in his hands and started to sob. 'I can't tell you, it's something that happened over thirty years ago and I try to blot it out of my memory.'

I was poleaxed. It couldn't be, could it? I pulled up on the hard shoulder. I was shaking and I could hardly breathe. He was unashamedly crying like a baby. Here sitting next to me in my car was the father of the two babies and the husband of the lady who had died in the fire that day thirty years ago, the memories of which are stamped indelibly on my brain. Here was the man who, because of odd circumstances, I'd never met, but had always wanted to. This was the poor man who had lost everything on that awful, fateful day.

'You're that Martyn, aren't you? Who was there on the day that I lost all my family.' And he threw his arms around me. We were both overcome big style but I managed to get off the motorway and onto a side road where I stopped and lit a fag. No one spoke, we simply couldn't and the tears and sobs were non-stop. We were both releasing emotions that had built up over thirty-odd years and exorcising our demons. Eventually we both calmed down a bit and James told me that after the funeral he couldn't cope and, within days, went to live down south. He later met a girl, remarried and had children.

About a year ago something was calling him back to the North and he later realised that that something was to try and find and then thank the people who desperately tried to help on the day of the fire and then attended the funeral afterwards.

'I only ever knew one name, Martyn Johnson, but thought I'd never find you. I only heard you on Cappo's programme once when I entered the competition and you were just known as Metal Detecting Martyn.'

We must have sat there for a good hour and we talked about the day in question and our 'if only' feelings. We never got to the metal detecting shop, it didn't matter any more. We just drove back to Sheffield in a state of euphoria. It was closure time for us both after more than thirty years. The coincidence of our meeting up as we did must be billions to one but it was just meant to be. Absolutely incredible.

James phoned the day after and asked if I would meet his new wife. I did so for half an hour and then we said goodbye with lots of thanks and hugs. I've never seen or heard from them since. I don't need to and I think they may be back down south.

'If only it had never happened in the first place.

*

This chapter has taken me longer to write than all the others put together. Until I met James I couldn't even talk about it and were it not for the amazing chain of events that brought us together again I could not have written it. Were it not for Cappo and BBC Radio Sheffield this closure would never have happened – thank you. I would like to dedicate this chapter to the unsung heroes of the Sheffield Fire Brigade.

CHAPTER TWENTY

Stories and Incidents

Little stories and incidents from my early days down The Cliffe make me realise how things have changed. My first shift was a night shift and, in those days, new recruits were shown round for three day or night shifts and then we were on our own.

It would be at about 2.30 am that I was asked by the desk sergeant at Attercliffe to go and sort out a problem at a private club on Amberley Place. It was my second night on my own and my fifth day in the force. It was a complaint by neighbours about the noise and should, I was told, be easy to deal with. When I arrived a few minutes later the music was blaring out and so I knocked on the door, which was fastened on the inside. The grille on the top half was slid open and I told the man who opened it of the complaint and told him to turn the noise down. The door slammed shut and after a few minutes' waiting I realised that the noise was just as loud. I tried again but with no result. After four tries later and with the noise level still as high I gave up and walked the 200 yards back to the nick.

Half a dozen of the old-timers were in the canteen and asked about the outcome. Even though I felt daft I told them the truth, I'd failed. No one spoke as half-full pint pots of tea and half-eaten sandwiches were left on the table. Helmets were put on and the big guys left the station and beckoned me to follow.

After a knock on the door the grille slid open to reveal the man I had spoken to earlier. With assistance from one of the big lads his head somehow came through the open grille, eyes bulging. As the grip exerted on the throat got tighter he somehow managed to open the door and in went the lads. The music stopped but I could hear the noise of tables over-turning and glass breaking and, every now and then, a body would fly through the open door and land on the pavement in front of me. You could tell from their faces that they must have had a 'little tiff' with someone and off they scuttled. A few minutes later the lads came out of the club and we all marched back to the nick in silence, where they finished off their snap. They didn't mess around in those days and the neighbours didn't make any further complaints. They didn't need to, the club never opened again.

One of the oddest crimes committed on a fairly regular basis throughout the city of Sheffield was the 'splitting' of a £1 or 10 shilling note (don't forget that in those days there was much more paper money than there is today – pound coins and 50p pieces were yet to be produced). Every now and again they would turn up at a shop, mainly newsagents'. The trick was to split the note into two halves so that each half showed either the front or the back of the banknote. This was then folded or rolled up and proffered to the shopkeeper with a request for ten Park Drive or Woodbine cigarettes. It was very ingenious and I once saw the offender do it whilst under arrest. It took less than ten seconds.

I couldn't see the point because wherever a spliced note turned up the police dealing with it would say, 'Gerald's out of prison again,' and go and arrest him. He would admit it and go back to prison once more. The poor man was the only one in Sheffield who could split notes and he became a victim of his own success.

Another unusual crime committed on a regular basis over several years involved Attercliffe police station itself. This always took place on the night shift, which each group worked roughly every three weeks. The desk sergeant and a clerk would man the office, which was situated on Whitworth Lane. In the early hours, usually between 2 am and 4 am, the front doors would open and a taxi driver would come to the front desk. 'I dropped a fare off here fifteen minutes ago and he said that he was coming in to get some money from his dad who works here on nights, but he's not come out yet.' There were very few people working and they were all asked but knew nothing about it and the taxi driver went without payment of the fare back to Sheffield city centre. It was assumed to be an isolated incident which nobody could reckon up until some time later, whenit was realised that it was happening fairly regularly and with whichever group happened to be working nights.

This went on for a year or two before Detective Constable John Longbottom saw someone walk out of the back door of the nick, which was on Howden Road. John knew the lad and, it being 3.30 am, grabbed him with suspicion. Sure enough, at the other side of the building in Whitworth Lane was a taxi driver looking for his fare and the lad was arrested. How audacious can you get. He knew that the nick was quiet at that time of the morning and, having left the taxi, he gently opened the station door, crept on his hands and knees under the office window, down the corridor, through the parade room and out of the garage door at the back and onto the next road, where he lived. Now that's what you call a cheeky pillock, using a police station as an escape route, but we couldn't help but laugh and admire his nerve.

One afternoon I was on duty at Attercliffe police station and, as I was passing the office, a man came in to report a crime.

'Officer, I've come to report a theft and it is most unusual,' he said.

'What is unusual to you, sir, I'm sure won't be to ourselves. Tell me what has happened.'

'This morning, just like every Saturday, my wife and I went into Sheffield shopping and we always catch the 2 pm bus back to Handsworth.'

I was tempted to say that when they got back the house had been burgled, but didn't.

'What happened then?' I replied, smugly.

'We live in a prefabricated house just off Richmond Park Road and quite a few people on the estate are being re-housed. When we left to go shopping the neighbours saw a removal van pull up and remove everything from the house.'

'Oh dear, why didn't they ring the police?'

'They assumed that we were also being rehoused and had forgot to tell them.'

'I'll take a report and make some inquiries, but it's certainly not that unusual – criminals watch for people with habits like your regular shopping trips on a Saturday and that's when they pounce, when they know that you will not be back until a certain time. I hope you're insured.' Again I asked quite smugly.

'We are, but I haven't finished yet.'

'What do you mean?'

'When the removal van left, a lorry turned up and the two men in it dismantled the house and drove away with it.'

'You must be joking.'

'I told you it was unusual, didn't I?'

This I had to see (or not see) for myself and I followed him back to the housing estate. The lawns and garden looked beautiful but something was missing – the house! The gardens and base were all that was left to see. The few neighbours left on the estate had all seen it happen but thought nothing was wrong, and the couple were left literally homeless until the council got involved. Our inquiries at local scrap yards and dismantlers were negative and I'm sure it will remain a mystery for ever. It certainly put a new slant on the 'House for Sale' column in the *Star* newspaper.

A good cuppa tea spot was worth a small fortune to us when working the beat and I had a good one at Slack's bread shop on Staniforth Road, near to Darnall Terminus. The two ladies who worked there, Vivien and Joyce, took pity on me because I was from Barnsley and lived away from home. I had many a sandwich and a pot of tea with them. Across the road was the Yorkshire Bank where the manager was Mr Fletcher, a nice man and I think originally from Blackburn. He called in every day for a sandwich and a piece of Bunnock (his words, not mine).

I was a customer at the bank and had had a letter or two from Mr Fletcher, asking when I was going to bank with them instead of them with me. I had exceeded my overdraft limit of £10. Because of this I was always very watchful when I left the shop in case he saw and collared me. On this particular day I was just about to leave the shop when Viv said to Joyce, 'Here comes Mr Fletcher for his usual.' The doorway to the back room was blocked by a large trolley full of bread so I was trapped. As the shop door slowly opened I flung myself to the floor behind the counter. Whilst I was out of sight of Mr Fletcher the shop got fairly busy. I must have lain there for fifteen minutes before I could get up and when I did I was covered in flour. It served me right and on the next payday, which was weekly in those days, I paid off my overdraft in full.

We were poorly paid then and I struggled to save any money. Ordinary police officers used to get 3s 9d per week (about 18p) boot repair allowance and about £10 per week pay. One of the lads was, supposedly, good at cobbling boots. On my two days off, I left my only pair of boots with him for repair in order to save some money. When I got back I was working days at Darnall with my newly repaired boots. No one had told me that PC Cobblers used to cut up old rubber car tyres and use them for the sole of the boots. I didn't mind being half an inch taller and I'd heard the expression finding your feet, but this was ridiculous. I managed to cross Greenland Road to the Terminus feeling a bit like Zebedee on the kids' TV programme *Magic Roundabout*, bouncing with every step. Once across the road I stood and watched the traffic with my feet apart and thumbs tucked under the buttons of my breast pockets to relieve pressure on the legs. All policemen rock gently backwards and forwards and I was the same. I rocked gently back on my heels, no problem, but as I rocked forwards the curve of the tyre coupled with the springiness of the rubber shot me forwards and I nearly bounced over the safety railings and into the road. Luckily I was on days and the shops were open so I had to go and buy a new pair of boots. Back in the red again already and I daren't call into Slack's sandwich shop for the next three weeks in case I bumped into Mr Fletcher from my bank.

A couple of days later I was working the beat at Grimesthorpe and took my old boots with me. I knew just the man for them. Everyone in the Grimesthorpe area knew Ronnie. He was a character.

Ronnie was about the same size as me and was always dressed in an old suit and a flat hat, which covered his bald head. No one knew how old he was including himself and today he would be classed as having special needs. I last saw him about five years ago and he looked the same as he did forty-five years earlier. He never aged. We all took a shine to Ronnie and he knew all our names. He used to watch us take the kids across the road to Earl Marshall School and then come and chat to us in his own peculiar way. He wanted to be a policeman and he sometimes walked the beat with us. If

Ronnie saw a child he would say, 'Be a good boy, be a good boy,' or 'Be a good girl, be a good girl.'

Ronnie had a wanted list, a police uniform, and he would say, 'Pocket book, Martyn, pocket book, Martyn,' or 'Whistle, Martyn, whistle, Martyn. Helmet, Martyn, helmet, Martyn.' He was the same with all the lads and not being able to help him was horrible. He used to cry loudly just like a three-year-old would. Ronnie lived in his own little world and the poor man hadn't got much going for him – or had he?

One day several of us got together, including a friendly police inspector, and we took Ronnie down to Attercliffe nick. He already had worn my old boots that I had given him and we managed to kit him out with a full uniform, pocket book, whistle and even a plastic toy truncheon and plastic toy handcuffs. He was beaming with delight and it didn't just make Ronnie's day complete, it made ours as well.

The police box at Grimesthorpe was where we kept our long white coat for when we took the school kids across the road and we said that Ronnie could keep his 'uniform' in there too. There was no such thing as political correctness or health and safety then, we used common sense and treated him like the human being that he was. The school kids knew him, pedestrians knew him and most of the drivers knew him. At school times he arrived for duty at the Tardis and donned his full uniform. Once we had stopped the traffic to enable the kids to cross the road PC Ronnie would join us in the middle of the road and wave the kids across and he, like us and everyone else, loved it and not once did anyone complain.

I'd not worked Grimesthorpe beat for a couple of weeks as it was the school holidays. PC Ronnie was waiting at the police box with his usual smiling face. 'Martyn, Martyn, miss you, miss you, letter letter.' He gave me several sheets of paper with wavy lines written on them – just like a proper letter.

'Thank you, PC Ronnie, I'll save them.' He put his arm round my neck and his head on my shoulder, patting my back at the same time, and simply said, 'Martyn my friend, Martyn my friend.' Ronnie's letter has been in my wallet from that day to this (about forty-five years) and it is one of my most treasured possessions.

Another little incident that I remember well involved a lad who, shall we say, had lost his way in life and decided to go on the road, living rough. The problem for us, the police, was that he couldn't cope with his decision to live rough and live off the land like most self-respecting tramps did. He couldn't skin a rabbit or pluck a hen, never mind cook them. As a result he became a thorn in the side of every bobby in Sheffield, breaking into cafés and stealing food. If a café reported a burglary any fingerprints were checked against his. About 70 per cent of the burglaries were down to him and he was circulated as 'wanted'. This went on for a year or two and he was always in and out of prison, usually for up to a month.

One morning I got a report that the Copper Kettle café on Attercliffe Common had been broken into and food had been consumed on the premises. A later examination of his prints against those found at the café showed it to be our Attempt to be a Tramp Man. I'd once shown him a map and explained to him how to get to Blackpool or Scarborough but this must have fallen on deaf ears and once more he was circulated as wanted. He could be anywhere but wherever he was caught it would be my job to fetch him back and I was hoping for a trip to St Ives or somewhere nice. A few weeks later he dropped (was caught) at, of all places, Wombwell, not far from Darfield where I was born.

At about 11.30 am on a Sunday morning in early December my mate Brian and I drove the short distance to Wombwell police station and arrested him. He was his usual laid-back self and readily admitted the offence.

On the way back to Sheffield I made a detour to call in and see my mum and dad at Darfield and also have a pot of tea. When we arrived they were glad to see us and my mum, Esther, was in the kitchen doing my dad's Sunday roast.

'Why didn't you tell us you were coming? We would have got a bigger joint.'

'We've just had a big breakfast, Mum, don't worry about

us,' I replied. Times were hard then and the little joint would barely feed them both. Just then Dad came into the kitchen, having been to look at the Panda car.

'What's that bloke doing in the back of the car?' he asked.

'He's a prisoner,' I said and quickly told them the story.

'Is he dangerous? He doesn't look it.'

'No, he's totally harmless, Dad, that's why he's not hand-cuffed.'

'Get him in here; poor lad can have a pot of tea and some biscuits.'

Mum's face was a picture when I brought him into the house and introduced him. As I took him into the front room to Brian and my dad, Mum whispered that he looked thin. We were all four chatting in the room and, after five minutes or so, my mum shouted laddo into the other room and the three of us kept chatting.

Ten minutes later Mum shouted Dad, Brian and me into the other room and told us our tea was out, and in we went. Sitting in Dad's chair was laddo and he was just polishing off Mum and Dad's Sunday dinner, joint and all. Dad's face was a study and I couldn't stop laughing.

'Fred, we're having corned beef sandwiches. That lad's starving,' Mum said. Dad pretended to be mad but I knew he wasn't.

'A man that nicks another man's snap deserves locking up,' Dad replied and laughed his head off. It made Mum and

Dad's day and they laughed about it for years afterwards. Laddo was happy and he wanted to be in prison for the winter months with a warm bed and plenty of snap.

Unfortunately for him, the judge was not pleased at his long string of convictions, particularly after the chances that had been given him. Laddo wished Mum, Dad and me a 'Happy Christmas' (and meant it) as he was led from the dock to the cells below. The judge wanted to teach him a lesson and gave him eighteen months, so at least he was out of our hair and out of the cold – for a while anyway.

I believe that we are all products of all our own experiences in life and several years ago someone asked me what my ambitions were. Because of what I have seen and dealt with, the answer came easily to me. To try and make ten people laugh a day and to try and do someone a favour a day.

I hope that you found the stories interesting. There are plenty more.

Thank you for reading them and I wish you all the very best.

Afterword

by
Detective Superintendent Paul Johnson
Queen's Police Medal (retired)

People wanting to become a police officer do so for three main reasons: some think of it as a nice, secure job; others believe that policing will provide them with an interesting and varied working life, with the possibility of promotion. The third group, by far the largest one, want to have the opportunity to provide a public service.

Martyn Johnson belonged to the latter group, one of the unsung heroes who do their job quietly, without fuss, in the service of 'their' community.

Like many jobs, policing can be routine and boring, but with periods of intense stress and excitement, tension and drama. Humour was, and still is, an important safety mechanism – a way of coping with often traumatic and debilitating events. Many people would view the occasionally dark humour used by many members of the emergency services as distasteful, without understanding the need for it, or the background to it.

Martyn patrolled the often unprepossessing streets of the East End of Sheffield, when a Health and Safety Risk Assessment meant checking your shoelaces before setting out on patrol. Counselling consisted of talking to your mates over a pint after work, and the height of technology was having a torch that worked!

The author describes himself as an 'ordinary working bobby'. Well, he was, but a darned good one. I am proud to call him my friend.

Enjoy his stories, and feel the mood of a working-class area in a vibrant northern city, where steel was still being produced, heavy engineering was state-of-the-art, and cutlery was world-renowned.